Soprintendenza per i Beni Artistici e Storici di Venezia

to my son Ezio

A better understanding and a fuller evaluation of the works in the Accademia Galleries have been made possible thanks in part to the excellent restorations carried out by the personnel of the Soprintendenza per i Beni Artistici e Storici di Venezia: Rosa Bagarotto, Chiara Maida, Alfeo Michieletto, Luigi Sante Savio and Gloria Tranquilli
Other contributions have been made by: Paola Borghese, Stella Foscarini Volpin, Ottorino Nonfarmale, Marica Petkovic, Walter and Valentina Piovan, Ferruccio Volpin, Marco and Serafino Volpin
Sincere thanks are due to Laura Barbiani, Roberto Fontanari, Sandra Rossi, Maria Destà for her collaboration

Translation
Ivor Neil Coward
Aaron Curtis
Nicholas Holland

www.electaweb.it

Reprint 2002
First Edition 1998

© Ministero per i Beni e le Attività Culturali
An editorial realization by Mondadori Electa S.p.a.

This volume was printed for Mondadori Electa S.p.a.
at Mondadori Printing Spa, Via Castellana 98, Martellago (Venice) in the year 2002

Soprintendenza per i Beni Artistici e Storici di Venezia

The Accademia Galleries in Venice

edited by
Giovanna Nepi Scirè

Electa

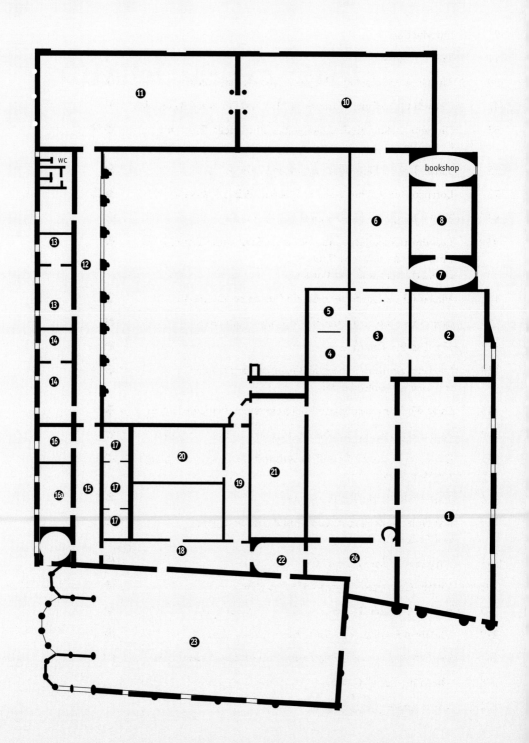

The Accademia Galleries

Introduction

In the early 1800's, the Galleries of the Accademia – containing the most important collection of 14th-18th century Venetian paintings – along with the Brera Picture Gallery and Bologna Accademia became a museum. Its political origins were, closely connected to the local events that in those years had reduced Venice to little more than a prize passed around among the great European powers. With the annexation under the Napoleonic Kingdom of Italy after the treaty of Presburg signed on December 26, 1805, and through Napoleon's decrees in 1806, 1808 and 1810, all the public palazzi and religious buildings were closed, and some were even destroyed. The works of art that surfaced from these events and which were somehow not sold or lost, found protection in the new Galleries.

Originally, however, the Galleries' purpose was largely educational, as is shown in the decree of September 1, 1803, extended on February 12, 1807 also to Venice, which established that – alongside an academy of fine arts divided into various faculties – there would be a gallery for the "benefit of those who practise painting".

The Venetian Academy of Fine Arts was forced to relocate from the *Fonteghetto della Farina* (flour warehouse) to a group of buildings – also acquired following the Napoleonic suppressions – which included the convent of the Lateran Canons, designed by Andrea Palladio in 1561, the Chiesa della Carità, reconstructed by Bartolomeo Bon between 1441 and 1452, and the Scuola della Carità, the first of the Venetian Scuole Grandi, founded in 1260. Thus there was also the problem of how to incorporate the works of art into structures whose original purpose was entirely different, and which were not connected to one another.

The Academy faced problems from the start, due to its relative distance from the city centre and its location on the other side of the Grand Canal. This situation was described in a painting by Canaletto now on display in the National Gallery of London, which shows, among other things, the *campanile* that has since collapsed. A further problem was the limited amount of space available for use without resorting to a vastly expensive remodelling project for the Palladio building. Nonetheless, the government's decision was unshakeable, and the Accademia – which had been considering the complex at Santi Giovanni e Paolo with its attached Scuola Grande di San Marco, or the Misericordia, or the church and monastery of Santa Caterina – found itself, instead, forcibly transferred to a location that was already recognised as completely inadequate.

The restructuring project was led by Giannantonio Selva and lasted until 1811. It was necessary to completely gut the church which, once the furnishings and altars were removed, was then divided horizontally and vertically to create five large rooms on the lower floor for the school and two on the upper floor to serve as exhibition rooms. These spaces were created

Canaletto, View of the Church of Santa Maria della Carità, *London, National Gallery*

Giuseppe Borsato,
Commemoration of
Canova in the Scuola
Grande della Carità,
Venice, Museo d'arte
moderna, Ca' Pesaro

after walling up the Gothic windows, with lighting coming from above. The
buildings were connected by opening a passageway on the first floor at the
back of the Sala dell'Albergo, and constructing a short stairway which led
through a foyer to the other rooms.

The Scuola della Carità underwent minor renovations, important work having
been carried out already during the 18th century under the direction of
Giorgio Massari and Bernardino Macaruzzi. In 1766 the ground floor entrance
had been completely remodelled, while a few years earlier the façade had been
renewed by opening the large doorway at the centre; this made the old stairs
obsolete, and they were demolished. In their place, two twin flights of stairs
leading up to the Chapter Hall (Room 1) were constructed based on models
by Macaruzzi. The small façade remained which connected the church and
school – and which served as the entrance to the school itself – in red marble
from Verona with the once coloured statues depicting *Virgin and Child with
Devotees,* by Marco Zulian (1345), and *Saint Christopher* and *Saint Leonard,*
(1378). The 14th century doorway in the courtyard is still intact, although it has
been walled in. It is topped by a coloured stone lunette with the symbol of the
Carità, commemorating the plague of 1348.

The rooms of the Scuola della Carità were largely left unaltered: the wooden
ceiling from the late 15th Century is still in the Sala dell'Albergo (Room 24),
as is the triptych by Antonio Vivarini and Giovanni d'Alemagna dated at
1446, and Titian's *Presentation* which dates from August 31, 1534 to March 6,
1539. The other canvases in the cycle – the *Marriage of the Virgin* by
Giampietro Silvio and the *Annunciation* by Girolamo Dente, are today in the
Parish of Mason Vicentino.

Also intact – aside from the fact that the altar was removed – is the great Chapter Hall (Room 1), where the sumptuous ceiling remains on display with its deep blue and gold lacunars, carved by Marco Cozzi from 1461 to 1484. Originally there were five high reliefs depicting the *Madonna della Misericordia* and the symbols of the other *Scuole Grandi*. They were removed in 1814 and disappeared thereafter, replaced today by the *Holy Father* at the centre which has been attributed to Pier Maria Pennacchi and was originally in the Venetian oratory of San Girolamo, and by the four *Prophets* by Domenico Campagnola also attributed to Stefano dell'Arzere, from the Scuola della Madonna del Parto in Padua.

It proved decidedly more difficult to adapt the Palladian convent, however, especially since its integrity had already been somewhat compromised by a fire in 1630. To provide greater exhibition surface Selva approached it with caution: the arcades of the Ionic loggia were closed leaving some half-moons for lighting; the windows on the Sant'Agnese canal were raised, and the cells on the top floor were modified to create the engraving school and lodgings for the professors.

Beginning on 10 August, 1817, the gallery was opened to the public for a brief period, and had a great number of visitors. A painting made by Giuseppe Borsato in 1822 commemorating Canova portrays with almost photographic precision how the first room must have looked at the Accademia's opening – with not only the Veneto paintings of the 16th century, but also Titian's *Assumption* from the Frari, which had been secured in 1816 by the president Leopoldo Cicognara.

The first items to be included in the collection were: a small number of works being, donations and trial works by the academicians which were brought over from the old Academy; some of the remaining paintings from the Scuola della Carità; Abbot Farsetti's collection of plasters, acquired from the Austrian government in 1805. Pietro Edwards was named the curator of the collection, had been in charge of public paintings from 1778 until the fall of the Republic. All the governments that followed in Venice found in him a highly competent and useful collaborator. He was employed by the French commissaries for the selection of the pieces to give to Napoleon in 1797, and performed a similar function under the Austrians and the Kingdom of Italy, at which time he received the title of "curator of state-owned holdings". However, the overlapping of responsibilities – at times contradictory – with the Accademia Galleries placed him in an ambiguous situation, and did not allow him to block the mass exodus of important pieces to Milan or the dispersion of many important works. Although the next secretary of the Accademia, Antonio Diedo, was responsible for choosing state-owned works destined for the Gallery itself, during the prolonged delivery period the more important works went to the Brera Gallery in Milan, while Titian's *Saint John the Baptist* was kept in Venice (in the church of Santa Maria Maggiore) only because of the mass outcry of the Venetian people. Luckily some paintings were added that France had returned, amongst which was Paolo Veronese's famous *Christ in the House of Levi*. Others were removed from Venetian churches, such as that of San Giobbe, and placed in the Accademia Galleries as a precautionary measure, and yet other paintings were added from the first private contributions to the Gallery.

Important works were added to the Gallery by bequest: in 1816 Girolamo Molin provided many works including an interesting group by early painters

Francesco Lazzari, Section of the tribunes with the project for the installation of Titian's Assumption *and Canova's* Thesus, *Venice, Corer Museum, Drawings and Prints Room*

that contained the *Stories of the Passion* from the Rimini school, triptychs by Alberegno and Jacobello del Fiore, the polyptych by Lorenzo Veneziano with the *Annunciation* and Giambono's *Paradise*. Canova's brother then donated the large plasters *Theseus* and *Hercules*. In 1833 (finalised in 1850) the bequest of Felicita Renier was added, with works such as *Saint Jerome* by Piero della Francesca, the *Madonna and Two Saints* and the *Madonna with Saints Catherine and Magdalene* by Giovanni Bellini, and Cima's *Deposition*. Lastly, in 1838 Girolamo Contarini donated his noteworthy collection of 188 paintings, which included Bellini's *Madonna degli Alberetti*, the *Madonna with Blessing Child* and the *Allegories*, Cima's *Madonna and Two Saints*, *The Wedding of Saint Catherine* by Boccaccino, the *Sacra Conversazione* attributed to Sebastiano del Piombo and six Venetian scenes by Pietro Longhi.

Some acquisitions – which were significant although relatively few considering the enormous availability on the market – further enriched the heritage. The collection nevertheless continued to favour and protect Venetian painting – as it does now – and so was not particularly suitable for a well-rounded artistic education. During the 1800's, much effort was made to balance out this situation until the end of the century, when interest in the educational aspect had all but vanished and with it the desire to expand the breadth of the gallery's collection.

Nonetheless, in 1822 the Accademia anticipated the intentions of the Brera Gallery and, through Abbot Celotti, acquired Giuseppe Bossi's prestigious drawing collection, which boasted more than three thousand pieces and included – in addition to folios by Leonardo da Vinci among which the famous *Vitruvian Man* – drawings from the Bolognese, Roman, Tuscan, Ligurian and Lombard schools, not to mention the German, French and Flemish schools that provided a certain uniformity to the collection of

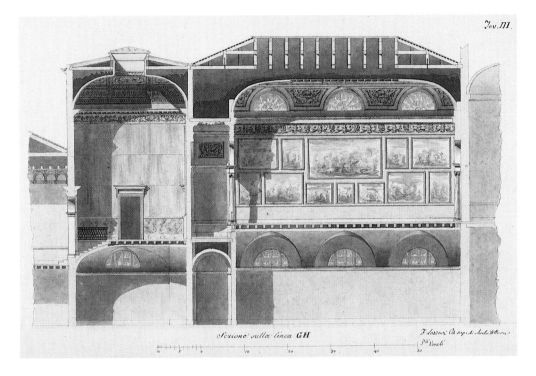

Sezione sulla linea GH

Francesco Lazzari,
*Section of the room used as
a picture gallery and of the
ground floor rooms, Venice,
Corner Museum, Drawings
and Prints Room*

paintings. Two years later, again through Celotti, a body of 602 drawings from Giacomo Quarenghi was secured.

As the number of art works increased, the exhibition spaces became wholly insufficient and overcrowded. The plans for enlargement designed by Selva, who died in 1819, were carried out under the supervision of Francesco Lazzari, and provided for two large halls to the left of the Palladian convent (Rooms 10 and 11). In 1828 both these halls were built, and the first one was opened; the second was not completed until 1834. Between the two halls four Greek marble columns, were transferred from the Scuola della Misericordia. In 1829 Lazzari completely remodelled the convent: in the courtyard he demolished the arches inspired by Palladian perspective and left intact by Selva, and expanded the ends with two intercolumniations. He reopened the walled up Ionic arches, which at a later time, along with the Doric arches, were fitted with large windows.

In 1830 the façade was also modified: the emblems of La Carità were replaced with those of the Accademia, windows were opened in the niches, and a sculpture – now in the Public Gardens – by Antonio Giacarelli of *Minerva Seated upon the Adriatic Lion* was placed at the top.

During this time, the large room on the ground floor was divided, giving the Galleries a separate entrance from that of the Scuola (shown also in Combatti's plan of 1847). It was also in this period that the painters and students of the Accademia decorated the lunettes on the ceiling of the first room with the portraits of the most important Veneto artists. Lastly, between 1849 and 1856, all the rooms were connected together, with the construction of the *sale nuovissime* (the "newest rooms", nowadays Rooms 6, 7, 8 and 9).

The collections were further expanded at this time, above all by the purchase from Emperor Franz Joseph in 1856 of several important paintings in the Manfrin Gallery, such as the *Madonna* by Nicolò di Pietro, *Saint George* by

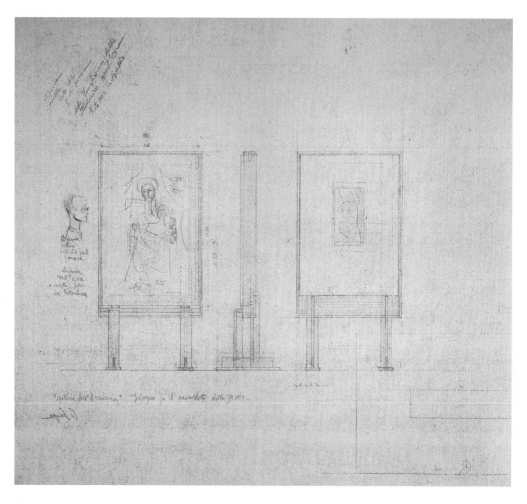

Carlo Scarpa,
Project for the awning for
the Madonna *by Paolo*
Veneziano, Room 1

Mantegna, Memling's *Portrait of a Young Man*, Giovanni Agostino da Lodi's *Lavander* and *La Vecchia* (*The Old Woman*) by Giorgione.

Initially, the annexation to the Kingdom of Italy did not bring about large scale changes but, from 1870 onwards, the school gradually became separate from the Accademia Galleries. This took place through various stages, including decrees in 1878 and 1879. The collection, entrusted to the supervision of the president of the Accademia, was officially delivered to him on January 15, 1881, while on March 13, 1882, final independence was sanctioned for both the school and the Accademia Galleries.

In 1895 the director, Giulio Cantalamessa oversaw a radical reorganization of the painting collection, including a new home for the *Assumption* (Room 2) based on a project by Giacomo Franco. By eliminating works by artists of the 1800's and consolidating the few paintings from other Italian and foreign schools, he tried for the first time to establish a chronological order. The unitary cycles from the 15th century schools of San Giovanni Evangelista and Sant'Orsola – formerly dispersed – were regrouped into two rooms of the church. The *Stories of Saint Ursula* were housed in a new octagonal space, with lighting from above, that would not actually replicate their original space (also due to insufficient information in that regard), but rather would serve to enhance the continuity of the pictorial narrative. 16th century Veneto paintings

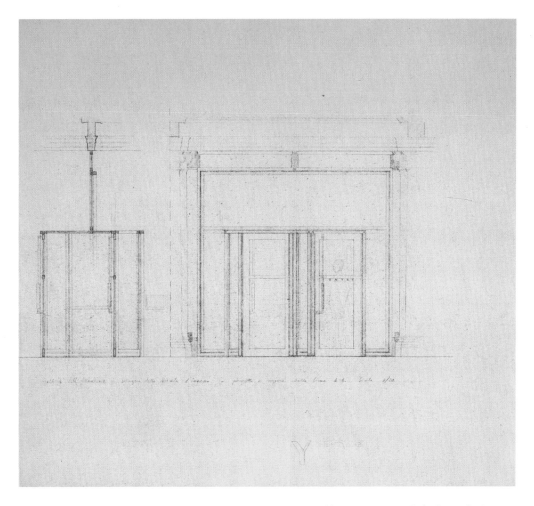

were placed in the large halls. Reacting probably to public opinion, Cantalamessa returned Titian's *Presentation* to the Sala dell'Albergo, where it had been located until 1828, believing correctly that it was preferable to respect the vision of the artist regarding the positioning and scanty lighting of the painting. The 18th century stone benches were then replaced with the 16th century dossals seen today. He also removed the bronzes, which were later brought together again in the Franchetti Gallery at Ca' d'Oro. Cantalamessa thus established what has remained the primary focus of the Accademia: a collection of Veneto painting from the 14th to the 18th centuries. Cantalamessa also enriched the collection, adding *Saints Peter and Paul* by Crivelli, works by Cosmè Tura, Basaiti's *Saint George*, Palma il Vecchio's *Sacred Conversation*, the *Wedding of Saint Catherine* by Lorenzo Veneziano, Paolo Veronese's *Hercules and Ceres*, and two early works by Tiepolo.

Cantalamessa was succeeded by Gino Fogolari in 1905, and little was done to the Accademia itself, although the collection of drawings and paintings continued to expand under his long direction, with the acquisition of two more early works by Tiepolo, various pendants, the *Death of the Virgin* by Pennacchi, the organ doors by Bellini originally at the Miracoli, Romanino's *Pietà*, the *Crucifixion of Saint Peter* by Luca Giordano, Strozzi's *Supper*, the *Portrait* by Fra' Galgario, Paolo Veneziano's *Madonna*, Tiepolo's draft of *The*

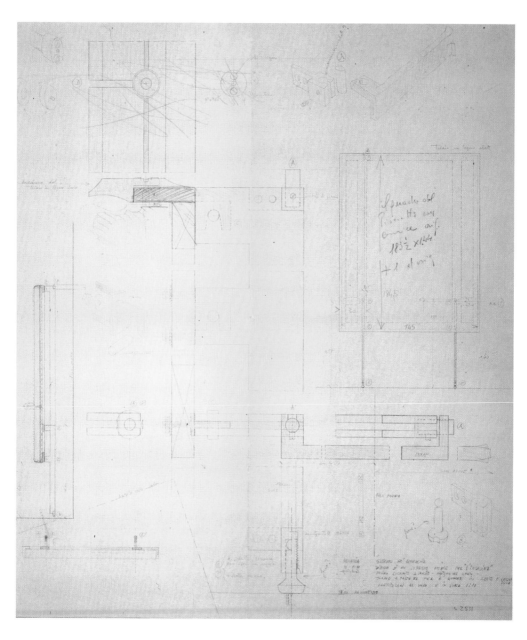

Carlo Scarpa, Project for the support for Giambattista Piazzetta's, The Fortune teller

Exaltation of the Cross, and lastly in 1932 Giorgione's *Tempesta*. After World War I, Fogolari lobbied for important pieces of art which had originally belonged to Venice to be returned from Austria.

During the war, the most important paintings had been kept in Florence. From 1921 to 1923, as these pieces were being returned, the museum was again remodelled.

The Accademia suffered the loss of Titian's *Assumption*, which was returned to the Church of the Frari; the room that had been designed for the large canvas seemed and remains disproportionate. The two rooms dedicated to the canvases of the *Ursula* cycle and the *Cross* cycle were eliminated, creating one large space with apses and restoring the truss ceiling and the Gothic windows on the side walls. The canvases with the *Miracles of the Cross* remained there, while the *Stories of Saint Ursula* were displayed in the small room where they are still kept today (Room 21): a largely arbitrary reconstruction of the room with choir stalls and backs from other locations.

A more 'original' arrangement was given to the rooms dedicated to the small 18th century works (Room 17), incorporating imitation materials and an antique door. 18th century doors, probably from a palazzo in Brescia and painted by Pietro Scalvini and Saverio Gandini, were purchased in 1912 and installed in the Palladian loggia, where they are still seen today. As under the direction of Cantalamessa, once again the works from the 19th century were removed and placed in storage at Ca' Pesaro; a similar fate awaited the paintings from foreign schools, which were moved to the Franchetti Gallery. The immediate need to implement more modern criteria for the museum reached its culmination during the 1940's, and especially after direction of the Accademia passed to Vittorio Moschini in 1941. Moschini worked with Carlo Scarpa even while World War II was underway to formulate a more articulate restructuring, including the construction of a large new building to add to the 19th century halls. The urgency to rebuild other Italian museums made it impossible to carry out the vast transformations that they had planned, but nonetheless a renovation project was begun which marked the end of a museum model that had remained unchanged since the turn of the century.

Work was begun in 1945 and lasted until 1960, involving the drastic elimination of the older rooms, carpeting, wooden skirting boards, imitation frames; these materials were replaced with a more neutral plaster with a special grain, warm-toned woods, jute, fustian, iron and glass, all carefully chosen and meticulously arranged. Given the space limitations and the fixed position of some of the larger canvases, a more logical itinerary through the museum was sought out, with a more careful selection of the works on display. The following year, the *Miracles of the Cross* paintings were re-grouped in a special room built in 1949 (Room 20) next to the hallway leading to the *Ursula* Room, and the two rooms – which were to house the closely related cycles – were connected by a small platform. As a result of this first project, which was improved later in 1959 and 1960, the room assumed its present appearance.

Also in 1947, the furnishing and arrangement of the *Ursula* room was completed, eliminating the previous design – which was completely anachronistic – and also that of the 18th century rooms, combining them into one larger room.

The following year, extensive imitation parts of the original wall decoration were removed from the church, and four new skylights were added to provide light from above. The 15th century paintings were arranged on panels, almost giving the appearance of a temporary exhibition, out of respect for the original architectural structure. Between 1950 and 1952 the first room was reorganised: the windows which had been walled in during the 19th century to increase the display area were re-opened , and some fragments of late 14th century frescos were revealed along the walls, while the view into the disproportionate room (originally for Titian's *Assumption*) was blocked with a wide brick panel where the *Lion* polyptych by Lorenzo Veneziano was to be placed. Between 1950 and 1953 the new entrance was created with its now famous compass, while in 1955 Rooms 4 and 5 were completed for the display of small sized masterpieces and Giorgione's *Tempesta*, finally removed from the isolated pre-war location.

Under the direction of Francesco Valcanover from 1961 to 1977, special attention was given to the improvement of services, from the most basic ones to the installation of new fire prevention and anti-theft systems. Further efforts were dedicated to the preservation of drawings, collected on the top floor in air-conditioned rooms and special cases. The museum was equipped with more rational and efficient storage facilities, while in the church in the room opposite the apses a space was created dedicated to Gino Fogolari for temporary exhibitions and shows. The collection did not grow in the years immediately after the war.

In 1949 Guido Cagnola generously donated a notebook of sketches by Canaletto depicting various Venetian scenes, an invaluable document for tracing the creative process in his paintings. Acquisitions were made again in the 1970's: in 1971 *Fire in the Oil Warehouse at San Marcuola* by Francesco Guardi was added, as was Mantegna's panel *Saint Peter and a Donor*, in 1979 Count Nani Mocenigo sold the large Longhi painting of *The Family of Procurator Luigi Pisani*; in 1981 the *Portrait of the Knight Giovanni Grimani* by Strozzi was obtained from palazzo Barbaro Curtis through a purchase option; in 1983 Jacopo Bassano's *Adoration of the Shepherds* was acquired from the Giusti del Giardino family. In 1987 two *Putti with Scrolls* and two allegories of *Justice* and *Patience* were obtained, remnants of the ceiling made by Giorgio Vasari in 1542 for a room in palazzo Corner on the Grand Canal. In 1983, after the death of Rodolfo Siviero – the former head of the office for the

Accademia Galleries, Room 9, visitor's facilities

recovery works of art "exported" to Germany before and during World War II, and to other countries in later years – Francesco Valcanolver successfully and courageously recovered at least thirty works from those that had been returned from abroad, and which had remained in Palazzo Pitti in Florence for decades while delivery plans were stalled and delayed.

Accademia Galleries, Church of the Carità view with the canvases of the Sala dell'Albergo of the Scuola di San Marco

Unfortunately the returned works were always fewer than those requested, but in 1988 seven paintings were obtained, including an episode from *Jerusalem Delivered* by Giannantonio Guardi, which was not previously in the Galleries, two small *Mythological Stories* by Sebastiano Ricci, and two *capricci* attributed to Canaletto.

In 1989 *The Great Wood* by Anton Francesco Peruzzini and Alessandro Magnasco was acquired through a purchase option. In 1995 Giuseppe Angeli's *Solletico* was acquired, and in 1997 thirteen large drawings by G. B. Piazzetta were obtained.

In 1988, after the exhibition on the restorations on Paolo Veronese's works, his ceiling pieces were displayed in Room 6. In 1994 a picture gallery was opened in the long corridor of the Palladian hall on the second floor, allowing for eighty masterpieces to be displayed which had originally been kept in the archives. In 1996 Room 11 was remodelled, and all the remaining pieces by Tiepolo from the destroyed ceiling of the Church of the Scalzi were placed there. Later, the Chiesa della Carità was completed, and the canvases which were previously in the Sala dell'Albergo of the Scuola di San Marco were displayed there. Fibre-optic lighting was installed in Rooms 4 and 5, and in the small gallery of 18th century paintings.

More recently, services were added in Room 9, but in spite of this the Accademia Gallery is still anxiously awaiting the acquisition of areas currently occupied by the Academy of Fine Arts in order to finally take its proper place among Europe's most important museums.

With regard to this introduction, see especially: S. Moschini Marconi, *Gallerie dell'Accademia di Venezia. Opere d'arte dei secoli XIV e XV*, Rome 1955; and E. Bassi, *Il complesso palladiano della Carità*, Milan 1980 and G. Nepi Scirè, *I capolavori dell'arte veneziana. Le Gallerie dell'Accademia di Venezia*, Verona 1991.
For the history of the collection of drawings at the Accademia Galleries, see also G. Nepi Sciré, *Storia della collezione dei disegni*, Milan 1982.

The "Primitives"

This was the room where the chapter met of the Scuola Grande di Santa Maria della Carità, the oldest of the six *Scuole Grandi* of Venice. These schools were powerful secular guilds for devotion and assistance to the poor. The ceiling, which was built between 1461 and 1484 by Marco Cozzi of Vicenza – at the time a member of the Scuola – is made up of square lacunars with leaf decorations on the side and heads of angels with eight wings, each with different facial characteristics. The blue background and the original colours of the figures have resurfaced from the gilt decoration made in the 1700s thanks to a long restoration project completed in 1992.

The paintings in the compartments, however, do not belong to the original decoration: at the centre is the *Holy Father*, probably the work of Pier Maria Pennacchi (1464–1514/1515), while at the corners are the four *Prophets* attributed to Domenico Campagnola or Stefano dell'Arzere (records from 1540 to 1575). The polychrome marble floor dates to the remodelling of the 1700s.

Paolo Veneziano,
Polyptych, detail

The rooms underwent other modifications in the early 1800s, when the entire complex of buildings became the Accademia: the back altar was removed, the windows were walled over to increase exhibition space and the original paintings were replaced with works that were to form the new gallery (including Titian's *Assumption*, now in the Church of the Frari). The present day configuration of the room is the work of Carlo Scarpa, begun in 1950. Scarpa reopened the windows, restored the fragments of late 14th century painting along the walls and arranged the gold backed paintings on the wooden panels with iron bases that still support them today.

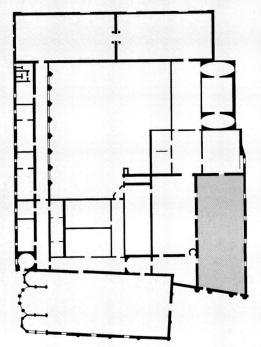

1a   1b   1c

1. Jacobello del Fiore
(recorded in Venice
from 1400 to 1439)

Justice and the Archangels
Panel, 208 × 194 cm
(central panel), 208 × 133
cm (Saint Michael),
208 × 163 cm (Saint Gabriel)
Acquisition: 1884,
following the Napoleonic
suppressions (cat. 15)
Latest restoration: 1997

Painted probably in 1421
for the seat of the
Magistrato del Proprio at
the Doge's Palace, which
oversaw the civil and
penal court. In the central
panel between two lions –
symbols of divine wisdom
– is Justice, who holds a
sword in the right hand
and scales in the left.
The closest iconographic
source for Saint Michael,
who holds up the scale
while slaying the dragon,
is found in a mosaic in St.
Mark's baptistery.
On the Latin writings
between the scrolls, the
archangel Gabriel entreats
the Virgin to guide men in
the darkness of their
actions, while Michael, the
warrior angel and defender
of the Church – in his dual
role as judge of souls and
fighter against the dragon, a
symbol of Satan – asks her
to levy rewards or
punishments according to
merit.
The wording behind

Justice "*I will carry out the
wishes of the angels and the
holy words, be mild towards
the pious, enemy of the evil
and disdainful of the proud*"
Is generally attributed in
Nordic art to Christ the
Judge.
Justice is clearly identified
with Venice, as it is also
featured on the relief of
the same period on the
west façade of the Doge's

Palace. The Venice–Justice
association, and that of
Peace is here enriched by
the Virgin Mary, since
peace and justice were
fundamental ideological
concepts of the Venetian
State.
This triptych was an
important official
commission for Jacobello.
Its complex symbolism
fully renders the spirit of

the Gothic with a
decorative aspect that
seems best defined as
"floral", as with
architecture and sculpture
of the time.
The piece was to be an
especially important
example for Michele
Giambono and Michele
di Matteo.

1

22

Paolo Veneziano
(active from 1333 to 1358 died before 1362)

2. *Polyptych*

Panels, gold background, 98 × 63 cm (central), 40 × 94 cm each (four side panels), 26 x 19 cm (above, six larger panels), 23 × 7 cm (above, four smaller panels), 30 × 16 cm (the two top panels)
Acquisition: 1812, following the Napoleonic suppressions. The central panel, which was taken to Brera by mistake in 1808, was united with the complex only in 1950, (cat. 21)
Latest restoration: 1951

At the centre, the Coronation of the Virgin. At the sides, the stories of Christ. On the upper part, at left: the Pentecost, Saint Matthew, the Vestment of Saint Claire, Saint John, Saint Francis gives his clothes to his father; at right, Saint Francis receiving the stigmata, Saint Mark, the death of Saint Francis, Saint Luke, Christ the Judge. At the centre: the two prophets Isaiah and Daniel.

The piece comes from the Church of Santa Chiara, as is attested by the Franciscan images in the upper part, and especially – in the *Death of Saint Francis* episode – the small monk, probably the commissioner of the work.

Dating to around 1350, the polyptych documents the insertion of mainland motifs into the Byzantine influenced culture of Venice, also revealed in the *Coronation of the Virgin* of 1324 in the National Gallery of Washington. These motifs become more complex here, with decorative effects and more accentuated Byzantine traits; indeed, the Byzantine influence in Paolo's work has led some to suggest that he travelled to Constantinople, where he obtained the new elements he would later introduce in his paintings.

The piece reveals great diversity between the small side episodes and the larger central figures, which are extraordinarily refined arabesques. This divergence does not, however, allow us to suggest that other hands were involved in the creation of the composition, especially given the consistently high quality of the work. The artist alternates the courtly and precious Byzantine language of the central part, with its fixed iconic nature that well suits the depiction of an event taking place outside normal time and space, with precise references to the western cultural affinity for the narrative unfolding of 'stories'.

3

3. *Virgin with Child and two Commissioners*

Panel, gold background, 142 × 90 cm, 157 × 105 cm
with the original frame
Acquisition: 1913 by purchase (cat. 786)
Last restoration: 1952

The piece was acquired in 1913 from the Salvadori antiquary of Venice. While the original two-tone 'toothed' frame and the old crossed support on the back are still intact, the work has lost the veiling of the flesh-tones, the lower inscription and some of the colours in the dress of the Virgin. It was first recognised as a work of Paolo Veneziano in the catalogue of 1928, and today it is unquestionably accepted as such.

Its similarity to the 1321 paliotto at Dignano, which the painting slightly postdates, points to its having been produced in the second half of the 1330s.

The Virgin with the infant Jesus in the clypeus constitutes a Syrian iconographic variant of the *Playtera*, while the gesture of sheltering the two small devotees, whose physical details make them veritable portraits, is an unusual reminder of the *Madonna della Misericordia*.

The monumentality of the image of the Virgin – "dark-faced like a Coptic or Cretan inspired icon" – and the harmonious assimilation of eastern and western elements, together with the humanity of the commissioners, make this arguably the artist's masterpiece.

2

1

1

4

of the artist's masterpieces for the transparency of its colours and the elegance of its figures. It was completed after 1427, when there was still a wooden crucifix on the altar. It is likely that the commissioner of the piece was the convent prior, Fra' Bernardo de' Scapi, who, like the artist, was also from Bologna.

5. Lorenzo Veneziano
(records from 1356 to 1372)

Saint Peter, Saint Mark

Panel, gold background, 115 × 42 cm, 115 × 64 cm
Acquisition: 1812, following the Napoleonic suppressions, (cat. 5, 5a)
Latest restoration: 1948

Signed and dated 1371, these are the side panels of a disassembled polyptych. The centre panel (the *Resurrection*) is kept a the City Museum of Milan. The association of the founder of the Church with the protector of the Venetian state and the fact that the work comes from the Silk Office at Rialto reveal the diffusion of religious devotion in the public life of the city.

6. Giovanni da Bologna
(records from 1377 to 1389)

Madonna dell'Umiltà, Saints and Members of the Scuola di San Giovanni Evangelista

Panel, gold background, 111 × 99 cm
Acquisition: 1812, following the Napoleonic suppressions (cat. 17)
Latest restoration: 1948

A work from the early 1380s. Connections between the artistic culture of the Venetian lagoon and that of the Emilia region are evident here, for example in the naturalism of the flowery meadow. Below, the members hold up the standard of the Scuola di San Giovanni Evangelista, where the painting originated.

4. Michele di Matteo
(documented in Bologna from 1410 to 1469)

Polyptych

Panels; the polyptych is made up of two orders separated by an overlying border 21 × 225 cm, and an overlying predella 38 × 225 cm. Each order is composed of three panels: 111 × 64 cm (upper middle), 142 × 63 cm (lower middle), and 11 × 85 cm (upper side), 142 × 85 cm (lower side).
Acquisition: 1812, following the Napoleonic suppressions, (cat. 24)
Latest restoration: 1979

On the lower order is depicted the *Virgin with Child and Four Angels*; to the left, *Saint Lucia and Saint Helena*; to the right *Mary Magdalene and Catherine of Alexandria*; on the pendentives are four panels with the *Doctors of the Church*. On the upper order at the centre is the *Crucifixion*; to the left the evangelists *Matthew and Mark*; to the right *John and Luke*. On the band separating the two orders in sixteen nooks are the *Redeemer* and Saints. On the predella are five stories about the discovery of the True Cross, from the left *Saint Helena arrives in Jerusalem, Saint Helena* convenes the Jews who keep counsel, Judas refuses to reveal where the Cross is, but after falling in a well he shows its location and he himself digs to find it, Proof of the True Cross which revives a small boy, Adoration of the Cross while the devils flee. At Saint Catherine's feet is the signature: "Michael Mathei da Bononia F."

This comes from the Church of Sant'Elena, where it was situated on the altar of Saint Helena, erected in 1418 by Alessandro Borromei. The frame is from the original complex, but was restored in 1829.

The work is considered one

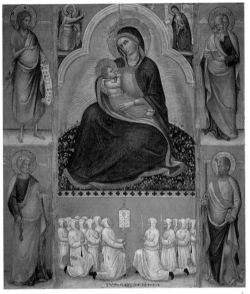

5a
6
5b

7. Veneto–Byzantine School – 14th Century

Virgin with Child

Panel, gold background, 77 × 38,5 cm
Acquisition: 1932, from the Duomo of Burano, (cat. 884)
Latest restoration: 1939

Panel originally in the Duomo of Burano. It is generally associated with the *Nursing Virgin* in the Marciano Museum but reveals a more accentuated Byzantine component.

8. Jacobello Alberegno (died before 1397)

Christ on the Cross, between the Virgin, Saint John, Saint Gregory and Saint Jerome.

Panel, gold background, 40,5 × 55 cm
Acquisition: 1816, bequest of Girolamo Molin (cat. 25)
Latest restoration: 1939

Dated to around the 1380s. The Virgin and Saint John are depicted at three quarter face, giving depth to the gold

background. The skull in the rocks at the foot of the cross is connected with an ancient Judeo-Christian cult for the burial of Abraham, a theme taken up often in 17th century sculpture and 14th and 15th century Tuscan painting.

7
8

9d   9c   9a   9b   9e

10

Lorenzo Veneziano
(records from 1356 to 1372)

9. *The Annunciation and Saint Gregory, Saint John the Baptist, Saint James and Saint Stephen*

Panels, gold backgrounds, 111 × 55 cm (central), 94 × 24 cm (sides)
Acquisition: 1812, following the Napoleonic suppressions, (cat. 9)
Latest restoration: 1988

On the step of the throne are the signature and the date of 1371. The original destination of the gold-backgrounded work is unknown. The use of the flowery meadow constitutes a new theme that would be widely developed by the International Gothic, and used previously by this artist in the panels in the Berlin Museum.

10. *Marriage of Saint Catherine*

Panel, gold background, 93 × 58 cm
Acquisition: 1900, donated by the Udine Seminary, (cat. 650)
Latest restoration: 1948

The artist's signature and the date of 2 February 1359 are visible below (according to the Veneto dating system, and therefore really 1360). The original location of the piece is unknown, but it is believed to have been the central part of a polyptych. Once owned by the Marin family in Venice, then it was acquired by Jacopo Danieli, passing on to Count Pellegrino of Zara, then to the Cernazai collection and finally to the Udine Seminary.

1

11. Catarino
(documented in Venice from 1362 to 1382)

Coronation of the Virgin

Panel, gold background, 89 × 60,5 cm
Acquisition: 1877, purchased from count Vincenzo Galli, (cat. 16)
Latest restoration: 1998

The work dates to 1375 and depicts Jesus and the Virgin seated on a single throne, placed against a background of the blue vault of heaven. In spite of the use of the same gestures and of rich colours the work appears less refined than Paolo Veneziano's treatment of the same subject.

12. Michele Giambono
(records from 1420 to 1462)

Saint James and Saints

Panel, gold background, 108 × 45 cm (central), 88 × 29 cm (sides)
Acquisition: 1812, following the Napoleonic suppressions (cat. 3)
Latest restoration: 1979

On the central part at the bottom is written: "Michael / Giambono Pinxit". Acquired in 1948 from the Scuola del

Cristo on the Giudecca island, but it originally belonged to the Chiesa di San Giacomo on the Giudecca. The saint appears in the central part and is represented by the staff and the book opened to a part of the epistles written to the apostle (I, 22), while to his right stands Filippo Benizi, the founder of the Serviti, with no halo because he was only canonised in 1671. Benizi appears holding the book of Psalms, opened to the verse "Servus Tuus sum ego".
As a late work from around 1450, it suggests an awareness, if not an understanding, of the Tuscan artists working in Venice, especially Andrea del Castagno, with his frescos in the chapel of San Tarasio at San Zaccaria. At the Albertina in Vienna there is a drawing with variations of Venerable Phillip and Saint Michael.

11

1

12

13

14

Savorgnan, then to Abbat Luigi Celotti who sold it to the Emperor of Austria for the new Imperial Museum in Vienna. It was assigned to the Galleries with the post-war restitutions (s. 18)

Originally from the Scuola Grande di San Teodoro. Composed of rock crystal and partially decorated with silver, the piece is housed in a case designed by Carlo Scarpa made of glass, iron and an antique fragment of porphyry. This object echoes the influence of the Tuscan artists working in Venice whilst retaining gothic elements of Nordic extraction.

15. **Venetian School of the Second Half of the 14th Century**

Coronation of the Virgin and the Stories of Christ

Panel, gold background, 55 × 39 cm (central), 55 × 41 cm (sides)
Acquisition: 1816 (cat. 23)
Latest restoration: 1951-54

At the centre, the Coronation of the Virgin; at the sides, the Stories of Christ: the Nativity, Christ with the Doctors, the Last Supper, the Crucifixion, the Deposition, the Resurrection, the Ascension and the Pentecost. The paintings are part of a single group of unknown origin which had been separated and was reassembled in 1954.

---

13. **Jacobello del Fiore**
(records from 1400, died in 1439)

Madonna della Misericordia with Saints John the Baptist and John the Evangelist

Panel, gold background, 87 × 114 cm

Acquisition: 1816, a bequest of Girolamo Molin, (cat. 13)
Latest restoration: 1987

Its original location is unknown. At the centre are the date and signature: "1436 Jachomello de Flor pense", which may also have been written on the frame, now lost. The date is clearly incorrect, however, as it does not correspond with the stylistic nature of the piece. Although the iconographical motif of the *Platytera Madonna* and the *Madonna della Misericordia* together was taken from Paolo Veneziano, the painting appears to owe more to the influence of Gentile da Fabiano and Michelino da Besozzo. It is a variation of a subject treated earlier, in 1407, on the Montegranaro triptych (today in a private collection in Switzerland). Comparison with the Montegranaro triptych reveals a moore subtle elegance, less iconic fixedness and even some studied characterisation of the small worshipers kneeling in the meadow covered with small flowers. The work probably dates to between 1415 and 1420. In fact, it bears a similarity

with the *Leone Andante* in the Doge's Palace, signed and dated 1415, and was clearly painted before the sumptuous *Justice* triptych, which is from 1421. Considering these factors, 1416 would be a more correct hypothetical date for the completion of the piece. With the removal of the 18th century frame, some fragments were found that had not been altered by light or varnishes, and some test brush marks.

14. **The 15th Century Venetian School**

The Cross of Saint Theodore

Rock crystal and partially gilded silver, 92 × 43 cm, bronze base 46 cm high
Acquisition: 1919, passed, with the Napoleonic suppressions, into the collection of Count

16d

16c

16. Jacobello Alberegno
(died before 1397)

Polyptych of the Apocalypse

Panels, 95 × 61 cm
(central), 45 × 32 cm,
45 × 33 cm, 44 × 33 cm,
45 × 32 cm
Acquisition: 1951, became
State property after the
Napoleonic suppressions. Five
panels moved to the deposit
of San Giovanni Evangelista
from where, in 1838, the
Vision and the *Judgement* were
sent on to Vienna and then
returned with the post-war

restitutions of 1919. Displayed
in the Museum on Torcello
until 1948. In that year they
were reunited with the
others which, since 1840, had
been in the Correr Museum.
Finally, in 1951 the whole
group was acquired and
displayed by the Galleries of
the Accademia (cat. 1000)
Latest restoration: 1952

The five panels depict one
of the visions described by
Saint John in the
Apocalypse, with the steps
marked by Roman

numerals. The central
panel shows Eternity in
Glory, with the lamb
between the four symbols
of the evangelists (IV),
with "six wings [...] and
full of eyes", adored by 24
elders; the side panels
depict *The Harvest of the
Earth* (XIV): "thrust in thy
sickle, and reap: for the
time is come for thee to
reap; for the harvest of the
earth is ripe" (14,5 -
16,1); Babylon (XVII), or
"the great whore [...]
seated atop a beast [...]
with seven heads and ten
horns" (16, 2 - 17, 8); the
Cavalcade of the Kings
(XIX): "And behold a
white horse; horse and he
who sat upon him [...] on
his head were many
crowns; and the armies
which were in heaven
followed him upon white
horses" (18, 18 - 19, 21)
and the *Final Judgement*
(XX): "I saw a great white
throne and him that sat on
it [...] And I saw the dead,

small and great, stand
before God; and the books
were opened [...]" (20,11
- 22,5).
On the book that Christ
holds open is written: "chi
no / n è scri / ti.su / questo /
libro // sera da / nadi".
Originally the work was
housed in the Church of
San Giovanni Evangelista
on Torcello, which fell into
ruin over the course of
only a few decades until it
was demolished.
The complex allegorical
theme performs its
didactic function with
great clarity, while the
figurative culture of
Giusto de' Menabuoi is
transposed in the more
typically Venetian terms of
chromatic sensibility and
expressive strength. The
Church of San Giovanni
Evangelista on Torcello
was reconstructed after a
fire in 1343, providing us
with a *post quem* date for
the work sometime in the
latter half of that century.

1

16a

16c

16b

17. Catarino
(documented in Venice
from 1362 to 1390)

*Coronation of the Virgin
and Angels*

Panel, golden background,
105 × 58 cm (central),
96 × 28 cm (sides)
Acquisition: 1902,
purchase of Tommaso
Mazzoli, (cat. 16)
Latest restoration: 1948

The original location of
the Triptych is unknown,
but it was probably
painted later than the
Coronation of the Virgin by
Paolo Veneziano of 1375
as is borne out by the
nonchalance of the
figures, the elegance of
Saint Lucia, inspired by
Lorenzo Veneziano, and
the rough features of
Saint Nicolas.

**18. Stefano "Plebanus"
di sant'Agnese**
(active from 1369 to
1385)

Coronation of the Virgin

Panel, golden background,
75 cm × 52 cm
Acquisition: 1816,
bequest of Girolamo
Molin, (cat. 21)
Latest restoration: 1951

The painting is signed
and dated 1381
("plebanus" means
parishioner). Although
the work is based on the
Coronation of the Virgin by
Paolo Veneziano, here it is
read with a full Gothic
sensitivity, evident in the
play of the perspective
planes and the use of
light and brilliant
colours.

19. **Antonio Vivarini**
(c. 1418/1420 – 1476/1484)

Virgin with Child

Panel, gold background,
64 × 41 cm
Acquisition: 1959, from
the parish of San Giorgio
delle Pertiche where it
had been deposited since
1846, (cat. 1236)
Latest restoration: 1958-59

The original location of
this devotional panel is
unknown. However, since
it came from state
holdings it must once
have been housed in a
public building, a theory
also supported by a 1711
inscription on the back
of the piece which refers
to a magistracy during
which time the work was
restored. The painting is
extremely contained, and
in spite of the retention
of the gold background it
reveals a knowledge of
new research on volume
and bright colours are
bright, techniques
proposed by the Tuscans,
and particularly
Masolino. It dates to
about 1440.

20. **Veneto School of the End of the 14ᵗʰ Century**

Portable Altar

Panel, gold background,
119 × 45 cm (central),
119 × 40 cm (sides)
Acquisition: 1812,
following the Napoleonic
suppressions, (cat. 14)
Latest restoration: 1950

On the central panel:
Madonna dell'Umiltà;
above: *Pietà*; at the sides:
the Saints James and
Francis, with the
instruments of the
Passion behind them. The
work dates to about
1385, and is from the
Chiesa di San Gregorio.

21. **Nicolò di Pietro**
(documented in Venice
from 1394 to 1427)

Saint Lawrence

Panel, gold background,
63 × 23 cm
Acquisition: 1816,
bequest of Girolamo
Molin, (cat. 20)
Latest restoration: 1951

Probably part of a lost
polyptych, the panel is
placed towards the later
phase of the artist's life.

19

20

1

21

31

23

22

22. **Nicolò di Pietro**
(documented in Venice from 1394 to 1427)

Virgin with Child

Panel, gold background, 100 × 66 cm
Acquisition: 1856, by purchase from the Manfrini collection, (cat. 19)
Latest restoration: 1949

Under the footboard of the throne is written: "hoc / opus / fecit fiei / dns vulcia / belgarcone / civis.ya / driensis / MCCCLXXXXIIII. Nichola / filus mri Petri pictoris de vene / ciis pinxit hoc opus qui mo / ratur in chapite pontis paradixi", which denotes the date of 1394, the name of the commissioner, the artist's signature and his address at the foot of the Paradiso bridge.
The earliest well known and dated work, the panel is so cohesive and refined that the question regarding the artist's previous training and production

has not yet been fully answered, nor has his role during the transition from Venetian painting of the 14th century to that of the 15th been adequately understood.
Compared with the abstract nature of Paolo Veneziano, the chromatic elegance of Lorenzo, and the decorativism of Jacobello, Nicolò stands out for his explorations in the use of colour and volume. As has often been stated, Nicolò looked significantly more towards the artists of the *terra firma* than to the figurative artists, noting such works as those of Alitichiero and Avanzo, the frescos in Treviso by Tommaso da Modena, and the works of Vitale da Bologna and other of his contemporaries in Bologna.

23. **Antonio Vivarini**
(records from c. 1418/1420 – 1476/1484)

Marriage of Saint Monica

Panel, 46 × 31 cm
Acquisition: 1816, bequest of Girolamo Molin, (cat. 50)
Latest restoration: 1951

Dated at around 1441, the panel was part of a series of Stories placed around a statue of Saint Monica in the Church of Santo Stefano. Below, a caption explains the depiction: "qui è como sancta Monika fu mandata a marito dal padre e da la madre" ("here it is shown how Saint Monica was sent to marriage by her father and mother"). Inspired by the style of Masolino and Paolo Uccello, the scene reveals new elements from the customs of the time and a studied use of perspective.

24. **Michele Giambono**
(records from 1420 to 1462)

Coronation of the Virgin in Heaven

Panel, gold background, 228 × 177 cm with gilded plaster decorations
Acquisition: 1816, bequest of Girolamo Molin, (cat. 33)
Latest restoration: 1949

Probably painted for the Church of Sant'Agnese around the middle of the 15th century, the panel repeats the same scheme and subject as that of Antonio Vivarini and Giovanni d'Alemagna at the Church of San Pantalon. Beneath the throne are putti who hold up the instruments of the Passion, while below them are the Evangelists flanked by the four Doctors of the Church. The surrounding space is entirely occupied by saints and orders of angels.

1

24

33

25. **Lorenzo Veneziano**
(records from 1356 to 1372)

Polyptych Lion with the Annunciation

Panel, gold background, lower order: 126 × 75 cm (central), 121 × 60 cm (sides); upper order: 82 × 83 cm (central), 67 × 30 cm (eight sides), 35 × 5 cm (36 small panels on the pillars)
Acquisition: 1812, following the Napoleonic suppressions, (cat. 10)
Latest restoration: 1997

At left, the saints Anthony (Abbot), John the Baptist, Paul and Peter. At right, saints John the Evangelist, Magdalene, Dominic and Francis. On the upper order, the Holy Father giving his blessing among eight Prophets. Below, on the predella, are the hermit saints Saba, Macarius, Paul, Hilary and Theodore. A work of very high artistic quality, it was originally on the high altar of the now demolished Church of

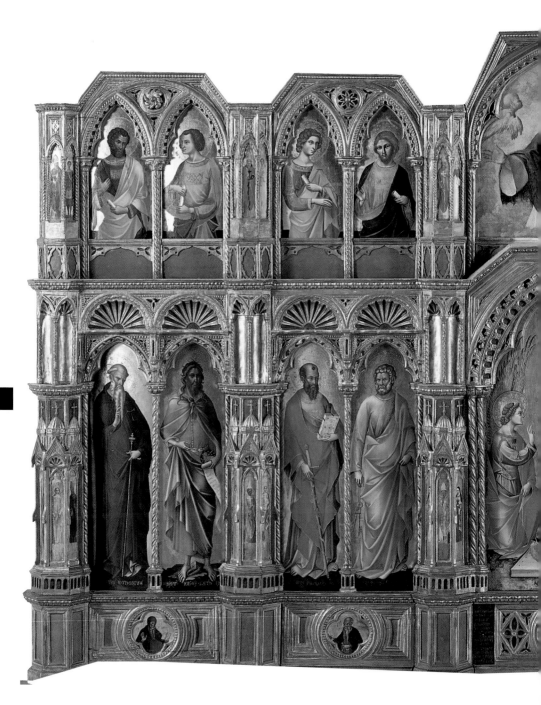

1

Sant'Antonio in Castello. On the inscription on the tablets at the sides of the central panel are written the date when the work was begun (1357) and the dedication to the commissioner Domenico Lion, shown to the lower right of the Virgin. The lower order – with its great Gothic elegance – is arranged according to a chromatic crescendo which begins with the dark tones of the side figures of Saint Anthony and Saint Francis and gradually reaches full chromatic luminosity in the central scene of the Annunciation. The upper panel in the centre is a replacement of the original, which was lost, and is possibly the work of Benedetto Diana.

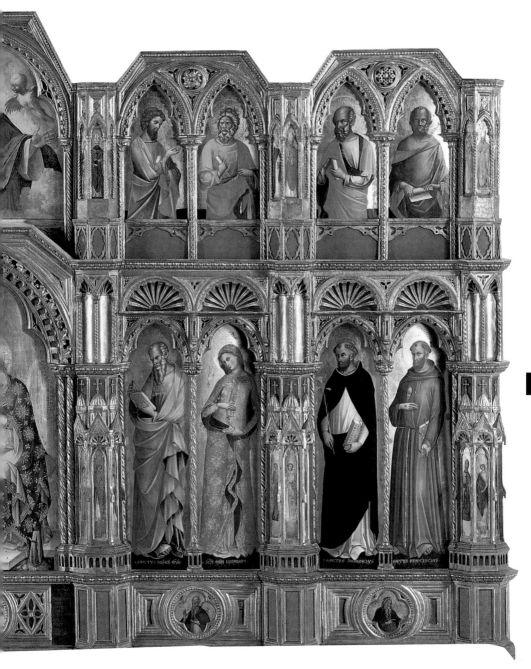

1

26d   26e   26f

**26. Rimini School
of the first half of the
14th century**

*Stories from the Passion of
Christ and the Universal
Judgement*

Panel, gold background,
17 × 14 cm each
Acquisition: 1816,
bequest of Girolamo
Molin, (cat. 26)
Latest restoration: 1979

These panels belonged to
the same group, together
with the five panels of
identical format in the
Staatliche Museen,
Berlin, and a *Deposition in
the Tomb* in a private
collection in Rome. The
panels were probably the
doors of a private
devotional diptych with
the Stories distributed on
three registers.
More recently, the
complex has been
attributed to Giovanni
Baronzio's early period.

27. Jacobello del Fiore
and assistants
(first half of the 15th
century)

Coronation of the Virgin
Panel, gold background,
281 × 302 cm
Acquisition: 1882, by
purchase from the Duomo
of Cereda (cat. 1)
Latest restoration: 1994-95

Dates to the first half of
the 15th century, the work
was commissioned for
Ceneda Cathedral by the
city's bishop, Antonio
Correr, who is depicted
kneeling at the lower
right. The crowded
composition provides a
more complex version of
Guariento's *Paradise* in
the Doge's Palace.

28. Jacopo Moranzone
(records from 1430, died
between 1467 and 1469)

Polyptych
Panel, gold background,
135 × 59 cm (central),
124 × 32 cm (sides)
Acquisition: 1812,
following the Napoleonic
suppressions, (cat. 11)
Latest restoration: 1952

On the central panel the
Assumption; on the side
panels Saints Helen, John
the Baptist, Benedict and
Elizabeth.
Originally in the Church
of Sant'Elena, where it
was painted with part of
a bequest established in
1441 by Donna
Elisabetta, the mother of
Fra'Tommaso da Venezia.
Sources indicate a
possible inscription with
the date of 1441, perhaps
on the now lost wooden
frame. Noted by Vasari in
1581 as the only work
worthy of mention by
the artist, who "made all
his figures on the points

of their feet".
The Gothic-like
composition, influenced
by Michele di Matteo's
polyptych for the same
Church of Sant'Elena,
indicates that the artist is
barely aware of the new
artistic ideas being
developed in Venice at
that time, while certain
roughness around the
edges reveal an aspect
typical in engraving,
which was an age old
tradition in the
Moranzone family.

27

28

The Great 15th Century Altarpieces, and Giovanni Bellini

This room was realized between 1886 and 1895 to house Titian's *Assumption* and other large altarpieces. After the *Assumption* was returned to the church of the Frari in 1919, the room appeared rather out of balance. To restore it's harmony, Carlo Scarpa replaced the decorated ceiling with a dark green plaster, replaced the polychrome marble floor with a dark grey Venetian style *terrazzo*, and created a new stairway to Room 3.

Giovanni Bellini, Virgin Enthroned with Child, *detail*

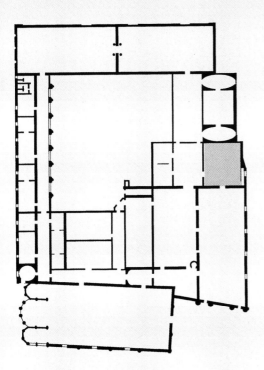

1. **Vittore Carpaccio**
(Venice? c. 1460-1525/26)

Crucifixion and the Apotheosis of the 10,000 Martyrs of Mount Ararat

Canvas, 311 × 204 cm
Acquisition: 1812, following the Napoleonic suppressions, (cat. 89)

Signed and dated 1515, painted for the Ottobon altar in the now demolished Church of Sant'Antonio di Castello. The altarpiece was probably commissioned by Enrico Ottobon, the grandson of the prior Francesco Ottobon, who had ended a plague at his monastery by invoking the 10,000 martyrs of Mount Ararat. 9,000 Roman soldiers, led by Acatio, were sent against the Armenian rebels and managed to defeat them only after an angel had told them to seek the help of Jesus, who led them to Mount Ararat, where he taught them about the Christian religion. Upon their conversion, the emperor approaches them with other pagan kings, threatening to make them suffer the pains endured by Jesus on the Cross. Their inyielding faith, even under torture, led another 1,000 pagan soldiers to convert and join up with the new Christians. During a violent storm, a final passion occurs, similar to that of Christ. The altarpiece brings various echoes together of the most modern culture of the time including suggestions of the woodcuts and paintings by Dürer which are in the Kunsthistorisches Museum in Vienna. In spite of a certain compositional virtuosity, it constitutes an extraordinary novelty in the field of Venetian religious painting. In fact, it replaces the usual votive representation of one or a few saints with a plurality of images, thereby depicting the collectivity of Christian virtue.

1

2. **Marco Basaiti**
(Venice, 1470/75-post 1530)

Prayer in the Garden with Saint Domenico, Saint Mark, Saint Louis of Toulose and Saint Francis

Canvas for transport from a panel, 369 × 222 cm
Acquisition: 1815, from the Church of San Giobbe, (cat. 69)
Latest restoration: 1987

At the foreground to the left on the ground is the fragmentary signature and the date of 1510. The altarpiece was originally in the Church of San Giobbe, on the first altar to the right belonging to the Foscari family. The composition follows a pyramidal scheme: the evangelical event takes place beyond the arc, while at the front are the eponymous saints of the Foscari family – Louis (Ludovic of Toulouse) and Francis to the left, Dominic and Mark to the right – presented as intermediaries between the faithful and the divinity.

2

3. **Giovanni Bellini**
(Venice, 1434/39-1516)

Madonna Enthroned with Child between Saint Francis, Saint John the Baptist, Saint Job, Saint Domenic, Saint Sebastian, Saint Ludovic and Angels Playing Music; known as the *San Giobbe Altarpiece*

Panel, 471 × 292 cm
Acquisition: 1815,
from the Church of
San Giobbe, (cat. 38)
Latest restoration: 1994–95

Originally in the Church of San Giobbe on the altar of Saint Job (Giobbe), the second one on the right. The large panel received great admiration from other artists at the time of its creation, and became a model for successive altarpieces. It has been shortened by 50 cm at the top. The presence of the apotropaic saints Sebastian and Roch indicates that the altarpiece was painted during a plague, probably the one of 1478. The niche, with its naturally proportioned figures composed in a pyramid, is almost a symbolic representation of the San Marco Basilica: the apse with the gilt mosaics, the stone wall panelling, the seraphs all allude to the Basilica. The triads of saints to the left and right of the Madonna are arranged in triangular patterns. In its original location, the illusion of depth was accentuated by sculpted pillars on the altar, faithful repetitions of those in the painting. The angels in the lower area playing the lute and the lyre are in honour of Saint Job, the patron saint of music.

2

3

4. **Vittore Carpaccio**
(Venice? c. 1460 – 1525/26)

Presentation of Christ in the Temple

Panel, 420 × 231 cm
Acquisition: 1815, from the Church of San Giobbe, (cat. 44)
Latest restoration: 1995

Signed and dated 1510, the altarpiece was originally in the church of San Giobbe in the third altar on the right (dedicated to the Purification of the Virgin), and was probably commissioned by Pietro di Matteo Sanudo. The presentation of the infant Jesus in the temple – forty days after his birth – occurs in a space in the shape of an apse, whereas the figures are all composed in a pyramidal arrangement. In addition to the extraordinary chromatic quality – recovered with the most recent restoration – certain aspects bear emphasising: the female faces inspired by the works of Pietro Perugino; the scenes from *Genesis* and the *Apocalypse* decorating the clothes of Simon, the priest; the three angels at the base playing the lute, lyre and *cromocorno*.
Considered to be a preparatory study for the two women's heads to the left of the Virgin, is a drawing in the Ashmolean Museum, Oxford, which was also used for the *Apotheosis of Saint Ursula* (Room 21, cat. 576).

2

4

5. **Giambattista Cima da Conegliano**
(Conegliano 1459-1517)

Madonna of the Orange Tree between Saint Ludovic of Toulose and Saint Girolamo

Panel, 211 cm × 139 cm
Acquisition: 1919,
returned from Austria,
(cat. 815)
Latest restoration: 1995

This signed altarpiece was originally to the right of the high altar in the church of Santa Chiara on Murano, and belonged to Franciscan monks. The presence of the Franciscan saint Ludovic of Toulouse, and the two monks about to enter the woods suggest that the work was commissioned by the same order. The theme is a variation on the "Flight into Egypt", an allusion provided by Saint Joseph and the ass in the background. The *sacra conversazione* thus takes place in a wide landscape, where certain symbols of Mary can be recognised, such as the city on the hill which recalls the birthplace of the artist, and rock which is also Mary's throne, and the orange tree after which the painting was named. The work dates to between 1496 and 1498.

2

5

6. Marco Basaiti
(Venice 1470/75-post 1530)

Vocation of the Sons of Zebedee

Panel, 385 × 265 cm
Acquisition: 1812, following the Napoleonic suppressions, (cat. 39)
Latest restoration: 1990-91

Signed and dated Marco Basaiti 1510, the work was once on the high altar of the Church of Sant'Andrea della Certosa. The most recent restoration revealed that the altarpiece was enlarged when the work was almost complete with the addition of the boats and the fisherman (Mark 1, 16-20), also with some corrections to the large figures in the foreground and to the background. The work was probably begun by Alvise Vivarini, but when this master died it was taken over and completed by Marco Basaiti, who worked in Vivarini's workshop at that time. The evangelical theme of the 'calling' is a clear reference to monastic life, also alluded to in various other sybolic motifs in the composition.

6

2

7

7. Giambattista Cima da Conegliano
(Conegliano 1459-1517)

Doubting Thomas with Saint Magnus

Panel, 210 × 141 cm
Acquisition: 1829, following the Napoleonic suppressions, (cat. 611)
Latest restoration: 1998

From the Scuola dei Mureri (masons) at San Samuele, with the Scuola's patrons, the saints Thomas and Magnus the Bishop, also depicted. The work dates to around 1504-05, immediately after the London version of the same subject, carried out originally for a confraternity in Portogruaro between 1502 and 1504. The episode does not unfold in an enclosed space, as the evangelical tradition would normally have it, but in an open loggia, with Saint Magnus taking the place of the usual eleven apostles. The careful use of shadows and light and the extraordinary compositional balance make this one of the most important of the artist's works of that time.

8

8. Giovanni Bellini and assistants
(Venice 1434/39-1516)

Mourning the Dead Christ at the Foot of the Cross (with Joseph of Arimathea, the Virgin and Magdalene, and Saint Martha and Filippo Benizi)

Canvas, 445 × 310 cm
Acquisition: 1829, following the Napoleonic suppressions, (cat. 166)
Latest restoration: 1964

Originally in the now demolished Church of Santa Maria dei Servi on the first altar to the right. The alter is dedicated to Saint Martha, depicted on the left along with Filippo Benizi of the servants of Mary, and not a part of the tradition of the Dead Christ removed from the cross. Their presence confirms that the altarpiece was commissioned by the Serviti friars, who rebuilt the altar in 1510, with the assistance of a group of tertiares from the same order. The painting also dates to about that time, and its very high quality – in spite of a previous attribution to Rocco Marconi – suggests that Bellini was largely responsible for the piece, with only limited intervention from his assistants.

9. Giambattista Cima da Conegliano
(Conegliano 1459-1517)

Virgin with Child and Saints

Panel, 414 × 209 cm
Acquisition: 1812, following the Napoleonic suppressions, (cat. 36)
Latest restoration: 1982

From the chapel of San Gregorio in the Church of Santa Maria della Carità. According to sources, the marble frame had been commissioned from Cristoforo Solari of Milan by the shipowner Giorgio Dragan, probably depicted in the features of Saint George. In the original location, the painting probably presented a strong spatial affinity between its painted architectural elements and the actual architectural structures surrounding it. The work was probably completed in around 1499, the date of the very similar polyptych by Miglionico.

2

9

Cima da Conegliano, Sebastiano del Piombo, Diana and Marescalco

This room was originally part of the Scuola della Carità, but was later called the Canova Room because it once contained a porphyry urn with his right hand, now located in the *tablinum*.
The casings of the windows were designed by Carlo Scarpa, probably when he planned the adjacent rooms.

Giovanni Bellini and assistants,
The Annunciation,
detail

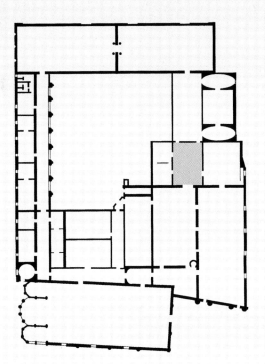

1a

1b

1. **Sebastiano Luciani, known as 'del Piombo'**
(Venice, 1485 – Rome, 1547)

Saints Louis, Sinibald, Bartholomew and Sebastian

Canvases, 292 × 137 cm, 292 × 137 cm, 292 × 136 cm, 292 × 136 cm
Latest restoration: 1984-85

These were the external and internal doors of an organ (now destroyed) in the Church of San Bartolomeo, displayed here until a definitive restoration of the original location is completed. Inspired by Giovanni Bellini and Giorgione, the paintings date to around 1508-09 and constitute the most important commission for the young artist.

2. **Giovanni Buonconsiglio known as 'Marescalco'**
(Montecchio Maggiore c. 1465 – Venice 1536/37)

Virgin with Child

Fresco, 313 × 200 cm
Acquisition: 1908, by purchase, (cat. 732)
Latest restoration: 1986-89

A removed fresco, originally in the Hierusalem Hospital in Montagnana (Padua), dating to between 1507 and 1513. It is the central part of a larger decoration that included saints in niches at the sides of the Madonna.

3

1c

1d

3

2

3. **Giambattista Cima da Conegliano**
(Conegliano 1459-1517)

Virgin with Child with John the Baptist and Saint Paul

Panel, 82 × 114 cm
Acquisition: 1838, donation from Girolamo Contarini, (cat. 603)
Latest restoration: 1979

Dates to the beginning of the 16th century. The face of the Virgin already reveals the typical characteristics of Cima's style, although the influence of Giovanni Bellini is still quite strong.

4. **Giovanni Bellini**
and assistants
(Venice 1434/39-1516)

*The Herald Angel
and The Annunciation*

Canvas, 225 × 105 cm, 225 × 105 cm
Acquisition: 1907, *The Herald Angel* by purchase; *The Annunciation*, withdrawn from the depository of San Francesco della Vigna, (cat. 734)
Latest restoration: 1998

The two paintings originally decorated the external doors of the organ of Santa Maria dei Miracoli; the internal doors had a Saint Peter (displayed in the Quadreria) and a *Saint Paul* (lost). The work has been attributed to various artists, including Carpaccio, as an external reference to the *Dream of Ursula*. Nowadays it is believed to be the work of artists working in Giovanni Bellini's circle, and based on drawings by the master. The marble pieces in the painting recall those of the interior of the Chiesa dei Miracoli, which was completed in 1489. This date signals the *post quem* period for the date of the paintings, which are probably from the last decade of that century.

4a

4b

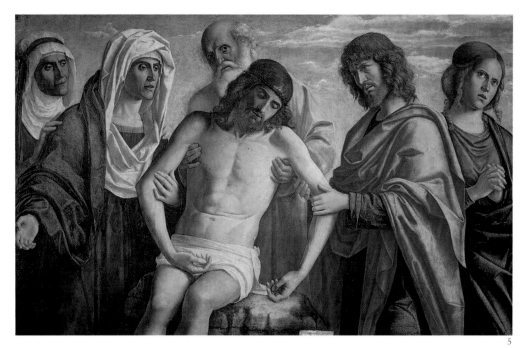

5

5. Giambattista Cima da Conegliano
(Conegliano 1459-1517)

Pietà

Panel, 70 × 113 cm
Acquisition: 1850,
bequest of Felicita
Renier, (cat. 604)
Latest restoration: 1990

Signed bottom-right, the
piece appears to be from
the younger period of
the artist's life (around
1490), as it has no
landscape details
whatsoever. The many
allusions to Alvise
Vivarini, Antonello and
Giovanni Bellini combine
to create a piece of great
balance.

6. Sebastiano Luciani known as del Piombo
ascribed to
(Venice 1485-Rome 1547)

*Virgin with Child, Saint
Catherine and Saint John
the Baptist*

Panel, 51 cm × 80 cm
Acquisition: 1838,
donation from Girolamo
Contarini, (cat. 70)

From the Contarini
collection, the piece may
have been commissioned
by a certain Caterina

Contarini, as the
inclusion of Saint
Catherine would
indicate. Although critics
are divided as to whether
the painting is by
Sebastiano del Piombo or
by Giorgione (or one of
his followers), the style of
the painting recalls the
early efforts of
Sebastiano, characterised
by the influence of
Giovanni Bellini and the
modern 'language'
employed by Giorgione.

6

7. Benedetto Rusconi, known as 'Diana'
(Venice 1460-1525)
The Virgin with Child and Saint John, Saint Louis and Saint Monica
Panel, 180 × 152 cm
Acquisition: 1832, probably following the Napoleonic suppressions,

(cat. 86)
Latest restoration: 1979

Originally on the altar of the sacristy in the Church of Maria dei Servi, where it was placed upon a lunette with the Holy Father, identified by some as the one set at the top of the large

polyptych by Lorenzo Veneziano (Room 1, cat. 21). It is a late work from around 1520, when the influence of Giorgione was enriched by experience with contemporary Lombard painting.

3

7

Giovanni Bellini, Andrea Mantegna, Piero della Francesca, Cosmè Tura and Giorgione

Carlo Scarpa redesigned these two rooms (4 and 5) in 1955, walling over their windows and making them into one open space divided at the centre by a panel positioned relative to the two pre-existing skylights. Works were shown using only original frames or frames of the same era; paintings which lacked a frame were inserted into wooden panels lined with material. For Giorgione's *Tempesta* brown velvet was used, the same as can be seen today.

Giorgione, La Tempesta, detail

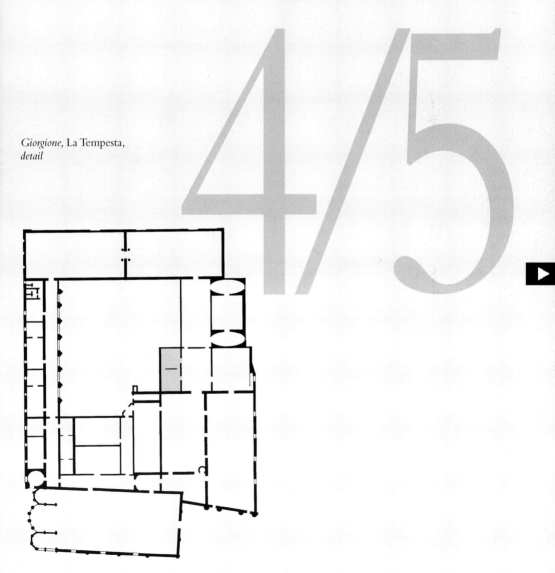

3. Piero della Francesca
(Borgo San Sepolcro, 1416/17-1492)

Saint Jerome and a Devotee

Panel, 49 × 42 cm
Acquisition: 1850,
bequest from Felicita
Renier, (cat. 47)
Latest restoration: 1948

The artist's signature "*Pietri de bu/go sci sep/ulcri opus*" (a work of Pietro di Borgo San Sepolcro) can be seen on the trunk of the tree where the cross is mounted. Although he has none of the traditional attributes, the devotee kneeling before Saint Jerome was recognised by a later inscription as the Venetian Girolamo Amadi di Agostino, originally of Lucca. The work was originally for private devotion, and dates to around 1450. A new, more balanced rapport between saint and worshiper is evident here, with the devotee portrayed in natural proportions. The landscape shows the homeland of the painter, San Sepulcro, and the Tiber Valley (although all the green components have unfortunately turned brown).

1. Giovanni Bellini
(Venice 1434/39-1516)

Virgin with Child

Panel, 77 × 57 cm
Acquisition: 1812,
following the Napoleonic
suppressions, (cat. 583)
Latest restoration: 1938

Traditionally identified as the *Madonna* which was once in the Palazzo dei Camerlenghi, the treasurers of the Venetian State, at the Rialto, although there is no trace of the gold background which that piece supposedly had. The painting dates to the 1470s and already reveals some of the typical traits of many Bellini Madonnas, where the influence of Mantegna – the artist's brother-in-law – is softened by a new sense of spirituality and humanity.

2. Andrea Mantegna
(Isola di Cartura, Padua, 1431 – Mantua1506)

Saint George

Panel, 66 × 32 cm
Acquisition: 1856, by
purchase from the Manfrin
collection, (cat. 588)
Latest restoration: 1992

Dated about 1446, this painting is believed to have been the side panel of a polyptych, but no confirmation of this has as yet been found. The stern young man – more mythical hero than Christian saint – wears a breast-plate inspired by a drawing of Jacopo Bellini, Mantegna's father-in-law. The fortified city in the background – also taken from a drawing by Jacopo – is a depiction of Selene, where according to the legend Saint George slew the dragon.

3

Jacopo Bellini
(records from 1424–1470/71)

4. *Virgin with Child*

Panel, 55 × 82 cm
Acquisition: 1829, it is
not known how this work
reached the Galleries,
(cat. 582)
Latest restoration: 1979

This work, already in
Padua at the end of the
18th century, in the
possessions of Abbot
Foscarini, was then
acquired by the engraver
Sasso. It is signed on the
original frame. Dating to
around the 1450s, it
belongs to the mature
period of Jacopo Bellini,
father of Giovanni. The
heads of the cherubs are
also found in some
drawings by the artist in a
book at the Louvre.

5. *Virgin with Child*

Panel, 63 × 47 cm
Acquisition: 1920, by
purchase, (cat. 835)
Latest restoration: 1994

The Madonna and the
Child are not painted
here in the traditional full
face manner of Byzantine
painting but rather at a
slight angle, and appear to
be engaged in a subtle
dialogue, an innovation
that places the work in
the mature period of the
artist's work.

4

5

6. **Cosmè Tura**
(Ferrara 1430-95)

Virgin with Child

Panel, 61 × 41 cm
Acquisition: 1896,
purchased, (cat. 628)
Latest restoration: 1982

A work by the master of the 15th century Ferrarese School of painting, dated between 1459 and 1463. This painting was probably conceived for a private residence, as the inscription near the bottom would indicate: "Sviglia el tuo figlio dolce madre pia / per far infin felice l'alma mia" ("Wake your sweet son, oh pious mother / and so make joyful my soul"). On the spandrel of the frame, two angels hold aloft the symbol of Saint Bernard, while the bunches of grapes with the goldfinches are symbols of the Passion of Christ. The small panel is also called *The Madonna of the Zodiac*, for the zodiacal signs traced in gold on the background; the signs for Acquarius, Pisces, Sagittarius and Virgo are still legible, while those to the right have all nearly disappeared. The presence of profane elements in a sacred painting, including references to astrology, reflects an intellectual custom of the time and is recurrent in Ferrarese painting.

6

Giovanni Bellini
(Venice 1434/39-1516)

7. *Madonna Enthroned Cherishing the Sleeping Child*

Panel, 63 × 120 cm
Acquisition: 1812, following the Napoleonic suppressions, (cat. 591)
Latest restoration: 1938-39

Damaged at the top. The painting is from the Doge's Palace (Magistrate of the Militia of the Sea), and was perhaps the central part of a larger group. In this work of the 1470s, Bellini again reveals his attentive observation of the contemporary figurative culture: the pose of the Madonna resembles the one in the polyptych by Bartolomeo Vivarini (Room 23, cat. 615), while the throne motif is taken from the Mantegna altarpiece of San Zeno in Verona.

8. *Virgin with Child and Saints Catherine and Magdalene*

Panel, 107 × 58 cm
Acquisition: 1850, bequest of Felicita Renier, following the Napoleonic suppressions, (cat. 613)
Latest restoration: 1997

Dated around 1500 (although some critics place it at about 10 years earlier), this painting reflects the influence of Leonardo da Vinci in its treatment of the relationship between background and subject, for example in how the side lighting makes the figures appear from the shadows. (In fact, Leonardo was in Venice during the year 1500s, sketching the portrait of Isabella d'Este.) Adorned with jewels and dressed with refined elegance, the two saints seem more like two young Venetian patricians than celestial creatures. A workshop copy of this piece is on display in Prado museum, Madrid.

7

8

9. **Hans Memling**
(Selingstadt am Main, c. 1440 – Bruges, 1494)

Portrait of a Young Man

Panel, 26 × 20 cm
Acquisition: 1856, by purchase from the Manfrin collection, (cat. 586)
Latest restoration: 1998

The portrait of the young man with his hair arranged in the 'Italian' style is exemplary of Memling's portraiture. Viewed from a three-quarters perspective and cropped at the shoulders, he is supported to the right by an invisible parapet in front of a landscape with trees. His pensive mien is revealed by the frontal lighting, while the sober clothing appears black today, but was originally a dark reddish brown. Dates to around 1480 or shortly thereafter.

Giovanni Bellini
(Venice 1434/39-1516)

10. *Virgin with Child and Saints Paul and George*

Panel, 65 × 88 cm
Acquisition: 1850, bequest from Felicita Renier, (cat. 610)
Latest restoration: 1939

In this work, which dates from the last decade of the 1400s, the artist varies the "Virgin with Child" theme derived from the well-known *Madonna degli Alberetti*; he wides the format, making it more horizontal, and inserts the two saints. Comparison with the head of Saint Paul in the *Coronation* in Pesaro reveals how the artist is now seeking a softer form. In spite of the expressive strength of Saint George – perhaps a portrait of the commissioner – and the compositional innovations, the work was probably completed with the help of assistants.

9

11. *Virgin with Child, John the Baptist and a Saint*

Panel, 55 × 77 cm
Acquisition: 1926, from the Giovanelli collection by special agreement with the State, (cat. 881)
Latest restoration: 1998

The work attests to the artist's attempt at the

beginning of the 1500s to insert figures taller than the usual half-bust into a more articulated space. It also reveals numerous corrections over the course of the painting. The gestures, the poses and the expressions of the images in the foreground

10

prefigure the Passion of the baby Jesus, depicted with his feet already crossed, just as they will be on the cross. The landscape in the background is full of Marian symbols such as the castle, the port, the fortress and the mountains, which – together with the christological elements – were intended to provoke the devout oration of the faithful.

12. *Pietà*

Panel, 65 × 87 cm
Acquisition: 1934, from the Donà delle Rose collection, following a convention, (cat. 883)
Latest restoration: 1996

A work commissioned for private use, Bellini's *Pietà* dates to the beginning of the 16th century and is signed near the bottom on the left side. It originally belonged to the Martinengo family who had it restored in 1866. The most recent

restoration revealed the well preserved paint. Careful analysis of the meadow and the image of Mary holding her dead Son suggest the influence of Dürer, or in any case of Flemish culture. Rich with religious symbolism (including the dry tree

covered in ivy and the small shrub to the left of Christ, symbols of Judaism and Christianity), the background landscape brings together buildings of various origin in suggestive synthesis, including the pre-Palladian basilica, the

duomo and the tower of Vicenza, a view of the Natisone at Cividale and the bell tower of Sant'Appollinare at Ravenna.

13

14

Giovanni Bellini
(Venice 1434/39-1516)

13. *Madonna of the Red Cherubs*

Panel, 77 × 60 cm
Acquisition: 1812, following the Napoleonic suppressions, (cat. 612)
Latest restoration: 1995

Painted in the late 1400s, this work was originally in the Scuola della Carità. The motif of the red cherubs is taken from the *Coronation* of 1474 in Pesaro. In the background – a luminous landscape rich with Marian symbols such as the hills, the river and the fortified city – Mary stares at her Son, almost enclosed in her hands, with tender awareness of his destiny.

14. *Madonna degli Alberetti* (*Madonna of the Trees*)

Panel, 71 × 58 cm
Acquisition: 1838, donated by Girolamo Contarini, (cat. 596)
Latest restoration: 1997

The first dated work by Giovanni Bellini (the date 1487 and Bellini's signature can be seen near the bottom in the centre, almost as if the foot of the small Jesus were pointing to them). The two trees at the side, which give the piece its name, may allude to the Song of Songs, or rather, given the dry shrubs at the sides of the trees, to the Old and New Testaments. The luminosity of the thin bands of landscape, the play between shadows and light, and the posture of the Mother allowing the devotee to observe her Son – barely covered by her delicate hands – make this one of the most moving works for private devotion.

15. *Virgin with Child*

Panel, 60 × 78 cm
Acquisition: 1838, donation from Girolamo Contarini, (cat. 594)
Latest restoration: before 1938-39

This may be the same *Madonna* that Taddeo Contarini left to his relative Girolamo in his will of 1578. Dating to 1480, the piece was created for private devotion and was copied in many variations by the master's collaborators; Giovanni himself would refer back to it some years later in his *Madonna degli Alberetti*.

15

Giorgione
(Castelfranco 1476/77–
Venice 1510)

16. *La Vecchia (The Old Woman)*

Canvas, transferred from
previous canvas, 68 × 59 cm
Acquisition: 1856, by
acquisition from the
Manfrin collection, (cat. 272)
Latest restoration: 1984

Like the *Tempesta*, *La Vecchia*
was also part of the
Vendramin collection, and is
quoted in its inventory of
1567–1569 and 1601. The
entry for 1601 also provides
a measurement of the frame,
which is still the original
one. The piece then passed
to the Manfrin collection,

although it is not known
when this occurred. The
interpretation of this work is
extremely controversial. It is
clearly an allegory, as the
writing on the scroll, "col
tempo" ["with time"],
would indicate, but despite
the symbolism, it is an
extraordinary portrait in its

own right. Dating to after
1505, it seems to reflect
certain ideas of Leonardo da
Vinci, evident in the dark
background, the impious
analysis, the gesture of the
hand pointed towards the
chest, similar to that of the
apostle Philip in da Vinci's
Last Supper in Milan.

16

17

17. **Giorgione**
(Castelfranco 1476/77-
Venezia 1510)

La tempesta

Canvas, 82 × 73 cm
Acquisition: 1932, purchased
from Prince Alberto
Giovanelli, (cat. 915)
Latest restoration: 1984

This painting has always
been identified with "*el
paeseto in tela con la tempesta
con la cingana et soldato, fu de
man de Zorzi di Castelfranco*"
("the landscape on canvas
with the gypsy and soldier
in a storm, by the hand of
Giorgione of Castelfranco"),
mentioned in 1530 by the
historian Marcantonio
Michiel in Gabriele

Vendramin's "camerino
delle anticaglie" (cabinet of
antiques). It is also indicated
in an inventory for
Vendramin's heirs in 1567-
69, and in another in 1601.
Then there is no mention
of the piece until 1855,
when it is recorded in the
Manfrin palazzo before
passing on to Prince
Giovanelli in 1875. Special
X-ray analyses have
revealed a nude woman
seated below the young
man, washing herself in the
pool of water to the left,
and numerous other small
corrections, especially in
the landscape. A work for
private enjoyment, the
Tempesta has been the

source of countless
interpretations, from
mythological to allegorical
and even political. It has
also been seen as the
melding of many literary

and figurative sources, or
even as a work which
would not require any
decoding whatsoever,
representing simply what
Michiel has suggested: a

18a

18b

"tempest" with a gypsy. The dating of the piece is also controversial, although it should be around 1505. Free from any graphic scheme and without the constricting support of a drawing, Giorgione constructs his images with overlapping veils of colour in a new chromatic-spatial synthesis, giving impetus to a more modern sense of painting.

Giovanni Bellini
(Venezia 1434/39-1516)
18. *Scroll* and *Head of Christ*
Panel, 33 × 22 cm
Acquisition: 1838, donation from Girolamo Contarini, (cat. 87)
Latest restoration: 1994

The two fragments (the signature appears on the second one) were probably part of a *Transfiguration*, perhaps the one which was once on the high altar of the Church of San Salvador, which however is also identified with the painting of the same subject kept at the Museo Correr. A new kind of humanity can be seen in the face of Christ, bringing it closer to the Baptism in Santa Corona, Vicenza, in the early 1500s.

19. *Allegories*
Panels, 27 × 19 cm, 34 × 22 cm, 34 × 22 cm, 34 × 22 cm, 34 × 22 cm
Acquisition: 1838, (cat. 595)
Latest restoration: 1979

Dating from the early 1500s, the panels were probably part of a piece of furniture with a mirror, used for holding toiletries. These were so popular as to attract the attention of the Senate, which prohibited their construction with a decree in 1479. The images that decorated the pieces were moral allegories that were supposed to make up for their frivolous destination. The woman with the sphere is perhaps a depiction of Melancholy or fickle Fortune; the nude with the mirror represents Vanity, and the reflection may be of the

commissioner; the image of Bacchus on a chariot offering a plate of fruit to a warrior is a reference to Lust, tempting the virtuous man; the allegory of Slander or Envy is represented by the panel with a seashell and a man with a twisted snake. The first panel – which was probably part of a different piece, or a replacement of a lost part – has been attributed to Andrea Previtali (Bergamo 1470/80 – 1528). It depicts blindfolded Fortune, set between two spheres, with two amphoras containing pleasure and anguish. This iconography was common in the Germanic tradition.

19a

19c

19b

19d

19e

63

Titian, Jacopo Tintoretto and Paolo Veronese

Part of the "*Nuovissima*" (very new) room connecting the old Scuola with Rooms 9 and 11, this room and the neighbouring rooms were built between 1840 and 1857. For a long time this was one of the poorest rooms in the Galleries, but in 1988, when the exhibition was held of Paolo Veronese's restored works, it was here that some of his great ceiling paintings were housed.

Veronese,
Venice Receiving Gifts
from Hercules and Ceres
detail

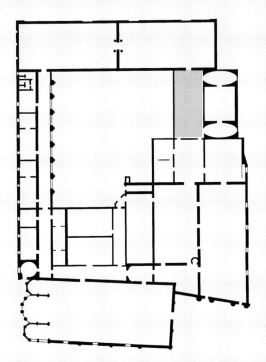

1. **Alessandro Bonvicino, known as 'Moretto'**
(Brescia c. 1498–1554)

The Madonna of Mount Carmel

Canvas, 272 × 298 cm
Acquisition: 1827, by exchange with the brother of Canova, who had purchased it in Rome, (cat. 321)
Latest restoration: 1988-89

On the scroll in the centre is written:"Divae Mariae Carmeli Societas". The large canvas was probably the standard of a Carmelite society: to the left of the Virgin is Saint Simon Stock, and to her right the blessed Carmelite, Angelo di Gerusalemme; they are surrounded by the commissioning members of the same institution, equally extraordinary portraits. Dating to around 1520-1522, this is one of the best works from Moretto's youth, with its realistic inquest into the traces of Foppa, Bergognone and Savoldo. This work could

1

be the "large canvas" that covered the image of the *Madonna delle Brine* in the Carmine Church in Brescia.

2. **Titian (Tiziano Vecellio)**
(Pieve di Cadore c. 1488/90–Venice 1576)

Saint John the Baptist

Canvas, 201 × 119 cm
(cat. 314)
Acquisition: 1808
Latest restoration: 1981

Signed "Ticianus" on the stone at the bottom, this painting was originally located in the church of Santa Maria Maggiore and after strong protest from the Venetians, the piece was entrusted to the Galleries rather than being transferred to the Brera gallery in Milan. The work follows a precise figurative programme in which "drawing", "colour" and "invention" are merged – almost a response to the Tuscan debate over whether Venetian artists were incapable of drawing well. The figure of the saint whose stunning preparatory sketch has

been revealed using X-rays – recalls both Michelangelo and classical art sources, while the background landscape is decidedly fresh and new. The work is from around the time of the *Presentation of Mary at the Temple* (Room 24, cat. 626), and the *Christ Crowned with Thorns* in the Louvre, which date to 1540.

Jacopo Robusti, known as 'Tintoretto'
(Venice 1519-1594)

3. *The Creation of the Animals*

Canvas, 150 × 258 cm
Acquisition: 1928, from the depository of the Doge's Palace, (cat. 900)
Latest restoration: 1967

4. *The Temptation of Adam and Eve*

Canvas, 150 × 220 cm
Acquisition: 1812, following the Napoleonic suppressions, (cat. 43)
Latest restoration: 1967

5. *Cain and Abel*

Canvas, 149 × 196 cm
Acquisition: 1812, following the Napoleonic suppressions, (cat. 41)
Latest restoration: 1967

6

2

3

4

5

These three works were created between 1550 and 1553 and were originally in the Scuola della Trinità, a school instituted by the Teutonic Knights near the Dogana da Mar (Custom-house), which was demolished in the 1600s for the construction of the Salute Basilica and rebuilt nearby. There were originally five paintings with the Stories of Genesis which were to complete the decoration of the Sala dell'Albergo, begun by Francesco Torbido. Of the five canvases by Tintoretto in addition to these, there is a fragment with *Adam and Eve before the Holy Father* at the Uffizi in Florence. In the *Creation*, the articulate forms of the other two stories become a painting composed almost like a tapestry, where a single vital breath seems to animate the Creator and his creatures. In the *Adam and Eve*, their naked bodies – arranged diagonally according to a refined mannerist technique – stand out against the dense mass of foliage. Adam and Eve are captured just before the consummation of their sin; to the right the sin has already been committed and the two progenitors are chased out by the angel. This is a fundamental work for the artist's treatment of landscapes. Also in *Cain and Abel* the figures are depicted against dense vegetation, which opens to the right onto an extraordinary piece of landscape, with the minuscule figure of Cain wandering in the distance. The scene recalls a similar subject by Andrea Schiavone in the Galleria Palatina in Florence, and especially the Titian painting of the ceiling of Santo Spirito in Isola, later transferred to the sacristy of the Salute Basilica.

6

6

7

Jacopo Robusti, known as 'Tintoretto'
(Venice 1519-1594)

6. *Saint Louis, Saint George and the Princess*

Canvas, 230 × 150 cm
Acquisition: 1937, from the ante-chapel at the Doge's Palace where it had been stored, (cat. 899)
Latest restoration: 1986

Like *Saints Jerome and Andrew*, this work was created for the first room of the Salt Magistrate in the Camerlenghi Palazzo at Rialto, and was commissioned by the magistrates Giorgio Venier and Alvise Foscarini who, upon completion of their service on September 13, 1551 and May 1, 1552, offered a votive painting for their office. The work was completed around 1552. In the composition, with its anti-conformist and unusual iconography, the female figure ardently rides the dragon in a posture of great virtuosity,

turning round towards the back and towards the saviour, mirroring herself in his bright breastplate. Saint Louis' pensive aspect makes a very effective side-scene. Tintoretto probably had some contact with contemporary theatre, and it may even be the case that he took inspiration from the set of Aretino's *Talanta*, designed by Vasari around 1542.

7. *Saints Jerome and Andrew*

Canvas, 230 x 150 cm
Acquisition: 1937, from the ante-chapel at the Doge's Palace, where it had been stored, (cat. 898)
Latest restoration: 1986

The painting was commissioned by the magistrates Andrea Dandolo and Girolamo Bernardo, who completed their service on September 6, 1552 and October 9, 1552. This last date provides us with a post quem date for the completion of the work, which was painted shortly after *Saint Louis, Saint George and the Princess*. The large cross painted transversely between the two nude bodies of the saints creates the optical illusion of extraordinary depth.

8. *Assumption of the Virgin*

Canvas, 237 × 135 cm
Acquisition: 1814, following the Napoleonic suppressions, (cat. 219)
Latest restoration: 1988
Originally in the demolished church of Santo Stefano the priest, known as San Stin, the work is usually dated to about 1550. The composition, with its dizzy swirling movement, reveals at least three portraits among the Apostles, probably the commissioners of the piece. The drawings on the back, with an altar, clearly refer to the original arrangement of the altarpiece.

9. **Paolo Caliari, known as 'Veronese'**
(Verona, 1528-Venice, 1588)

Venice Receiving Gifts from Hercules and Ceres

Canvas, 308 × 327 cm
Acquisition: 1895, from Palazzo Reale, (cat. 45)
Latest restoration: 1986

Originally on the ceiling of the Corn Magistrate's room in the Doge's Palace, in 1792 it was brought to the Marciana Library. In 1810 it was moved to the ceiling of the Napoleonic wing, and then later to the Accademia. The format of the painting, perhaps rectangular originally, was altered, probably in conjunction with its first transfer. It dates to around the same time as the canvases in the Collegio room of the Doge's Palace, and especially *Venice with Justice and Peace* of 1576-1578. A fundamental work of the artist for its crafted use of perspective and counter-lighting and its chromatic refinedness.

6

9

10

**Paolo Caliari
known as 'Veronese'**
(Verona 1528–Venice 1588)

10. *San Francesco Receiving the
Stigmata*

Canvas, 256 × 432 cm
Acquisition: 1919, returned
from Austria, (cat. 833)
Latest restoration: 1986

11. *Saint Nicholas, Recognised
as the Bishop of Myra*

Canvas, diam. 200 cm
Acquisition: 1817,
following the Napoleonic
suppressions, (cat. 661)
Latest restoration: 1986

These paintings originally
decorated both the ceiling
of the demolished church
of San Nicolò della Lattuga
at the Frari, together with
the *Adoration of the Magi* at
the centre and the four
Evangelists at the corners
(these five paintings are
now on the ceiling of the
chapel of the Rosary at the
church of Santi Giovanni e
Paolo. The *Saint Nicholas*
painting was once four-
lobed, like the *Saint Francis*,
but was made circular to be
set in the central space of
the ceiling of the first room
of the Galleries. The two
canvases represent the
artist's style in the 1580s,
incorporating a darker

palette in spite of the airy
depths furrowed by light
clouds, and significant
attention to perspective.
The paintings were
completed near the time of
the re-consecration of the
church, which took place
in 1582.

12. **Paolo Caliari,
known as 'Veronese'**
and assistants
(Verona 1528–Venice 1588)

Assumption of the Virgin

Canvas, 464 × 310 cm
Acquisition: 1818-21,
following the Napoleonic
suppressions, (cat. 541)
Latest restoration: 1988

The large canvas
decorated the ceiling of
the refectory of the now
demolished San Giacomo
convent on the Giudecca,
flanked by two ovals with
the *Annunciation* and the
Visitation (in storage), and
surrounded by a frieze
with leaves, putti and
figures (most of this in
storage). On the back
wall was the *Feast at the
House of Levi* (stored at
the Verona City Hall),
probably by Benedetto.
Although this is a late
work, and a collaboration
– as been stated by

various sources –
Veronese is surely
responsible for much of
the actual painting and its
scenic creation with the
mannerist arbour, which
has its origins in works
by Correggio or
Parmigianino.

13. **Paolo Caliari,
known as 'Veronese'**
(Verona 1528–Venice 1588)

Coronation of the Virgin

Canvas, 405 × 219 cm
Acquisition: 1812,
following the Napoleonic
suppressions, (cat. 264)
Latest restoration: 1969

Originally the altarpiece of
the high altar of the
Church of Ognissanti in
Venice which was
consecrated on July 21,
1586, the date which
should also correspond to
the paintings completion.

11

This is one of the artist's later works (a study for a sketch preserved at Christ Church in Oxford), which critics have recently held to be almost entirely the work of the artist himself. The coronation of Mary is not a part of the evangelical tradition, but was a very common devotional element at a popular level. The Virgin is crowned by the Holy Trinity in the presence of angelic choirs, the Evangelists, Apostles and all the saints, to whom the church was of course dedicated ("Ognissanti", "All Saints").

14. *Penitent Saint Jerome*

Canvas, 253 × 168 cm
Acquisition: on deposit from Sant'Andrea della Zirada
Latest restoration: 1988

Kept on deposit from the Church of Sant'Andrea della Zirada, which was closed in 1971. Originally it was to the right of the high altar. This painting also belongs to the mature phase of the artist's work, as is shown by the beautifully rendered nude and the quality of the wide landscape to the right of the saint's home. It is marked by the usual attributes: the domesticated lion, the crucifix, the skull, the books, the cardinal's hat hung on the trunk. Dating to the end of the 1570s, this is a later example of a theme treated by Veronese in 1566 for the Church of Santa Maria degli Angeli on Murano (now at San Pietro Martire), and in a painting at the National Gallery in Washington.

12

6

13

14

Lorenzo Lotto, Romanino and Jacopo Palma il Vecchio

Along with Room 6, these two rooms (with the third as an extra service room) are part of the "*Nuovissima*" (very new) wing of the Galleries that was constructed between 1845 and 1875.

The rooms were remodelled by Carlo Scarpa in 1949. Prior to this, in 1933, Room 7 was lined in green velvet and had been reserved for two works by Giorgione: the famous *Tempesta*, and the *Nude*, a fragment of the Fonte dei Tedeschi frescos, today on display in the Galleria Franchetti at Ca' d'Oro. Scarpa added some false walls to the room, thus creating a slightly trapezoid layout.

Lorenzo Lotto,
Portrait of a Gentleman in his Study, *detail*

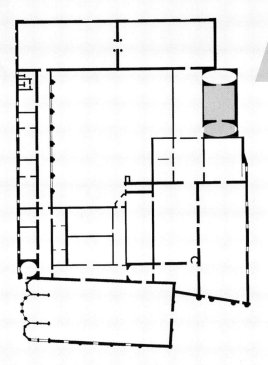

1. **Giovanni Busi, known as 'Cariani'**
(Venice, 1485/90-still living in 1547)

Portrait of a Man

Canvas, 68 × 56 cm
Acquisition: 1850, bequest from Felicita Renier, (cat. 299)

Completed around 1517, this portrait recalls the Giorgione-influenced culture in its use of colour, and in the expression and pose of the subject.

2. **Antonio Badile**
(Verona 1518-1560)

Portrait of Friar Salvo Avanzi

Canvas, 65 × 57 cm
Acquisition: 1957, by purchase option, (cat. 1318)
Latest restoration: 1958

This portrait, influence by Lotto, is signed and dated on the back "M. D. XXX. XVI." It depicts Avanzi with the attitude and symbols of Saint Thomas Aquinas, whose Dominican order the friar belonged to.

3. Giovanni Girolamo Savoldo
(Orzinuovi? 1480–c. 1550)

Saints Anthony Abbot and Paul the Hermit

Panel, 165 × 137 cm
Acquisition: 1856, purchase from the Manfrin collection, (cat. 328)
Latest restoration: 1997

On the stone at the bottom is the signature and date, perhaps decipherable as 1520. It is the first dated work of the painter, who appears to have been aware of the innovations of the Tuscan painters and the texts of Dürer and Leonardo da Vinci, but where an almost pre-Caravaggio Lombard element is particularly noticeable.

4. Alessandro Bonvicino, known as 'Moretto'
(Brescia 1498–1554)

Saint John the Baptist and Saint Peter

Panels, 114 × 50 cm, 113 × 51 cm
Acquisition: 1856, by purchase from the Manfrin collection, (cat. 332, 331)
Latest restoration: 1959

Early works, whose chromatic scheme and silvery coldness reveal the artist's Lombard origins, although enriched by his experience in Venice.

Bernardino Licinio
(Poscante c. 1490–Venice c. 1565)

5. *Portrait of a Lady*

Canvas, 68 × 60 cm
Acquisition: 1850, bequest from Felicita Renier, (cat. 303)

At the base, the two coats of arms with lions holding up the sun and the moon, belong perhaps to the Morello family of Treviso. From the 1540s, the portrait appears to imitate Paris Bordon's studies in colour and form.

6. *Portrait of a Lady*

Canvas, 47 × 45 cm
Acquisition: 1838, donation from Girolamo Contarini, (cat. 305)

A fine example of 16th century portraiture, this work is characterised by a warm tonality and studied psychological introspection.

4a 4b

5

6

7

7. Lorenzo Lotto
(Venice c. 1480–Loreto
1556)

*Portrait of a Gentleman in
his Study*

Canvas, 97 × 110 cm
Acquisition: 1930,
purchase, (cat. 912)
Latest restoration: 1997

Painted between 1528 and
1530, this is one of the
most famous portraits by
Lotto. The young
melancholie man is
captured as a thought
distracts him from his
reading; his pallid face
emerging from the
darkness reveals a
psychological intensity
that foreshadows modern

portraiture. On the table,
the rose petals, ring, letters
and small lizard probably
allude to the transience of
life, and perhaps to an
unhappy and lost love.

**8. Jacopo Negretti,
known as 'Palma il
Vecchio'**
(Serina near Bergamo
1480–Venice, 1528)

Assumption of the Virgin

Panel, 192 × 137 cm
Acquisition: 1812,
following the Napoleonic
suppressions, (cat. 315)
Latest restoration: 1993

From the Scuola di Santa
Maria Maggiore. The
painter received 50 ducats

on 5th February, 1513 for
this piece. Two episodes are
depicted on it: the
Assumption of the Virgin
and the legend of the
waistband that she will give
to Thomas as proof of her
rise to heaven. The Mary
we see here is not
extended upwards, but
rather turned in a human
gesture towards the small
figure of the Apostle
coming towards the mount
to witness the event.

**9. Titian (Tiziano
Vecellio)**
(Pieve di Cadore
1488/90–Venice 1576)

Saint John the Almsgiver

Canvas, 262 × 153 cm

Latest restoration: 1989-90

From the Venetian church
of San Giovanni
Elemonsinaro, where it
will be relocated once
restoration of the edifice is
complete. The saint's
clothing is formed of tight
folds of blinding
brightness, and he appears
seated at the centre of a
diagonal which passes
from the beggar below to
the left to the youth
holding the cross to the
right. The sumptuous
quality of the colours date
the piece to around 1550,
when Titian began to
explore that "chromatic
impressionism" that would
posit colour over form.

8

9

10. Jacopo Negretti, known as 'Palma il Vecchio'
(Serina, near Bergamo 1480-Venice, 1528)

Holy Family with Saint Catherine and Saint John the Baptist

Canvas, 126 × 195 cm
Acquisition: 1900, by purchase, (cat. 147)
Latest restoration: 1956

One of Palma's masterpieces, which remained unfinished at his death but was brought to completion by Titian, who painted the head of the saint and the landscape with the castle, as X-ray analyses have shown.

10

11

12

11. Titian (Tiziano Vecellio), ascribed to
(Pieve di Cadore 1488/90-Venezia 1576)

The Archangel Raphael and Tobias

Panel, 170 × 149 cm
Acquisition: 1812, following the Napoleonic suppressions, (cat. 1325)
Latest restoration: 1994

From the church of Santa Caterina. Below at the centre is the Bembo coat of arms. Cleaning has brought to light the extraordinary quality of the work, leading recent critics to suggest that it was painted by Titian.

Bonifacio de' Pitati, known as 'Bonifacio Veronese'
(Verona 1487-Venice 1553)

12. The Eternal Father and Saint Mark's Square

Canvas, 165 × 130 cm
Acquisition: 1919, following the Napoleonic suppressions, (cat. 917)
Latest restoration: 1991

Originally the piece was the central part of a triptych, whit the *Herald Angels* at the sides and the *Annunciation* (on display in the Quadreria) from the Camerlenghi

Palazzo at Rialto. The presence of the Loggetta of the campanile – completed by Sansovino in 1540 – provides a *post quem* date for the work, being around 1543-1544. The view of Saint Mark's reveals certain particulars of a slice of Venetian life: in the foreground to the left a furrier's shop, near the campanile a group of acrobats, and in front of then the porters.

14a

14b

13

13. *The Madonna of the Tailors*

Canvas, 129 × 149 cm
Acquisition: 1945, from Palazzo Reale, (cat. 1305)

Signed and dated 1533, the work was originally on the altar of the Scuola dei Sartori (Tailors' School), with its symbol of a large pair of scissors, here depicted at the feet of the Virgin. To the left, Omobono, the patron saint of the tailors, gives alms to a cripple: it is a clear message of charity to the more wealthy members of the Scuola.

14. **Giorgio Vasari**
(Arezzo 1511-Florence 1574)

Justice
Panel, 77 × 185 cm

Putto with Scroll
Panel, 77 × 65 cm

Putto with Scroll
Panel, 77 × 65 cm

Patience
Panel, 77 × 182 cm
Acquisition: 1987, by purchase, (cat. 1370, 1372, 1373, 1371)
Latest restoration: 1989-90,

These paintings come from the ceiling of the Corner Spinelli Palazzo on the Grand Canal. The decoration was completed in 1542 and included nine paintings (such as the allegorical figures of Faith, Hope and Charity), now dispersed among various collections or lost. The putti with scrolls are inspired by high-reliefs presently at the Archaeological Museum, but which were once on the walls of a building in Saint Mark's Square. The figures are silhouetted, projecting out from an invisible parapet against the deep sky, perfecting

an idea of Pordenone on the lost ceiling of the Scuola di San Francesco at the Frari. This work attracted considerable attention from Venetian artists, particularly Paolo Veronese.

14c

14d

15a

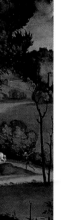

15b

15. **Andrea Previtali**
(Barbenno, Bergamo
1470/80–Bergamo 1528)

Nativity

Canvas, 132 × 215 cm

Crucifixion

Canvas, 132 × 215 cm
Acquisition: 1897, by
exchange from the
Church of the Redentore,
(cat. 639, 640)
Latest restoration: 1982

Dating to between 1515
and 1520, these early
paintings were perhaps
originally in the Doge's
Palace. The admiration
for Giovanni Bellini and
Lorenzo Lotto is evident.

16. **Girolamo Romani,
known as 'Romanino'**
(Brescia 1484/87– c. 1556)

Deposition

Panel, 183 × 185 cm
Acquisition: 1909, by
purchase, (cat. 737)
Latest restoration: 1975

An early work, signed
and dated 1510,
originally in the Church
of San Lorenzo in
Brescia. In addition to the
important elements taken
from Bellini, Giorgione
and Titian, there are also
significant Lombard
components, which in
their entirety form a
balanced synthesis of
form and colour.

17. **Venetian School of
the 16ᵗʰ century**

Visitation

Canvas, 209 × 150 cm
Acquisition: 1814,
following the Napoleonic
suppressions, (cat. 95)
Latest restoration: 1955,

Originally in the
monastery of
Sant'Andrea, this work
was attributed to many of
the great masters of 16th
century Venice. The
setting appears typical of
Giorgione, while the
figures recall Sebastiano
del Piombo, but any
further or more certain
attribution is not possible.

16

7/8

17

Titian, Jacopo Tintoretto and Paolo Veronese

Begun by Francesco Lazzari in 1828, the room was inaugurated in 1834. The passage between this room and its twin hall (Room 11) is decorated with four columns in Greek marble from the Scuola di Santa Maria della Misericordia.

Tiziano, Pietà, *detail*

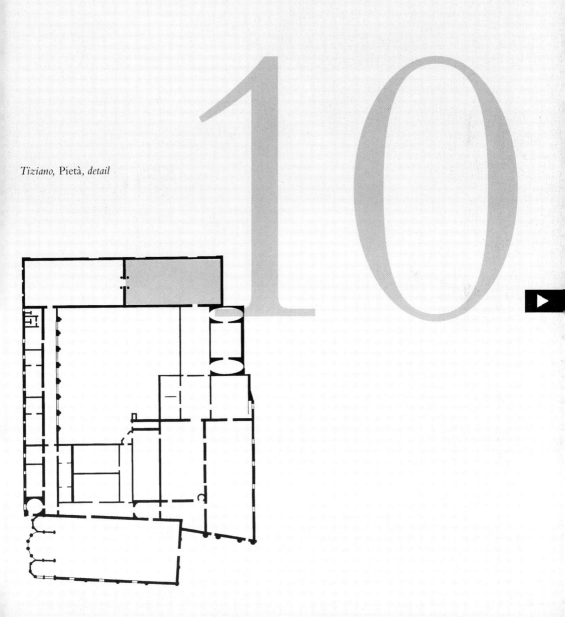

1

Paolo Caliari, known as 'Veronese'
(Verona 1528-Venice 1588)

1. *Virgin with Child and Saints*

Canvas, 338 × 187 cm
Acquisition: 1817,
following the Napoleonic
suppressions, (cat. 37)
Latest restoration: 1969-70

Originally on the altar of
the sacristy of the church
of San Zaccaria, the work
was taken to Paris in
1797 and then given to
the Accademia in 1815 in
exchange for three
paintings which are still
in the church. In 1562
Francesco Bonaldo
undertook to pay 200
ducats to refit the sacristy
and the altarpiece should
date to slightly later,
around 1564. The artist
appears particularly
interested in the
relationship with the
environment where the
painting was originally
kept, an aspect which is
of course now lost. The
mannerist elements
present here work
harmoniously and with
an almost classical sense
of balance, evidence that
Veronese had taken in the
great devotional tradition
of the 15th and 16th
centuries explored by
artists from Giovanni
Bellini to Titian.

2. *Christ in the House of Levi*

Canvas, 560 × 1309 cm
Acquisition: 1815,
following the Napoleonic
suppressions, (cat. 203)
Latest restoration: 1980-82

This great painting,
which was taken to Paris

3

and then returned in 1815, was originally a *Last Supper* for the refectory of the convent of Santi Giovanni e Paolo, as a replacement for a *Last Supper* by Titian which had been lost in a fire. According to the writing at the base of the pillar bottom left, the work was completed on April 20, 1573, but three months later the artist was accused of heresy for this vast composition which contained what were considered to be excessive anti-conformist elements. In spite of his strong defence of his artistic freedom, Veronese was ordered to "correct" the painting at his own expense within three months. But the only change he made was to

add the writing on the top of the pillar with the date below, clearly at the suggestion of Dominican scholars: "fecit D. Covi Magnum Levi – Luca Cap. V", so as to avoid scandal. In fact, Luke says in chapter V of his Gospel: "Levi held a great banquet for the Lord". In the work, with its triple-arch background inspired by the buildings of Palladio and Sansovino, Veronese's research into the idea of the banquet is concluded, with the attainment of a complete balance of scenic elements and figures.

3. *Allegory of the Battle of Lepanto*

Canvas, 170 × 137 cm
Acquisition: 1812, following the Napoleonic suppressions, (cat. 212)
Latest restoration: 1983

Originally in the Church of San Pietro Martire on Murano, to the right of the Rosary altar, while to the left was the *Madonna of the Rosary*, dated 1573 (Quadreria cat. 207), completed by the workshop based on a Veronese drawing. In the lower area is depicted the battle of Lepanto of 1571, which was between the Lega Santa and the Turkish Fleet, which was also commemorated by prints at around that time. On the upper part is Venice between Saint

Mark and Saint Giustina, on whose feast day the battle took place. Venetia is shown being presented to the Virgin, while to the left Saint Peter and Saint Roch intercede for her. The small canvas, clearly by the artist himself, was perhaps commissioned in 1573 as an *ex voto* by Pietro Giustinian of Murano, who had distinguished himself in the battle, or by Onfrè Giustinian who brought news of the victory to Venice.

2

Jacopo Robusti known as 'Tintoretto'
(Venice 1519-1594)

4. Transport of the Body of Saint Mark

Canvas, 397 × 315 cm
Acquisition: 1920, from the Salone Sansoviniano of the Libreria Marciana, (cat. 631)
Latest restoration: 1991-92

Painted between 1562 and 1566 for the Scuola Grande di San Marco (where the three paintings below are also from, while a find one with the *Discovery of the Body of Saint Mark* is in the Brera gallery in Milan), paid for by the Guardian Grande Tommaso Rangone. The

work attests to Tintoretto's extraordinarily imaginative and evocative style, and reveals the new *luminismo* which typifies Tintoretto's paintings from this period.

5. Miracle of Saint Mark Freeing a Slave

Canvas, 416 cm × 544 cm

Acquisition: 1821, with the works returned to Venice from Paris, (cat. 42)
Latest restoration: 1965

This was the first painting made by Tintoretto for the Chapter Hall of the Scuola Grande di San Marco. Brought to Paris in 1797, it was returned in 1815 and

4

5

entrusted to the Accademia Galleries. It was probably commissioned in 1547 and completed by April of 1548, when Aretino praised the work in a letter to Tintoretto. The scene is of a condemned slave being freed as a result of the intercession of Saint Mark. The slave was to be blinded and have his legs broken because – against the wishes of his master – he had gone to worship the relics of the saint. In this work, with its remarkable new dramatic effect and intense use of colour, the various figurative phases of the artist are summarised, especially the Michaelangelo-influenced aspects, rendered through a methodical graphic effort, in a vision of such newness that it could only provoke wonder and bewilderment from his contemporaries.

6. *Rescue at Sea*

Canvas, 396 × 334 cm
Acquisition: 1920, from the Salone sansoviniano of the Libreria Marciana, (cat. 832)
Latest restoration: 1992-93

Painted between 1562 and 1566, this painting depicts the miraculous rescue of a Saracen sailor who at the turn of Alexandria had called upon the saint during a storm. The painting is composed of two pieces which reveal transparent pencil sketches on the back, with no relation to the final composition but which indicate how Tintoretto used different fragments of canvas. This work is especially fascinating for its dramatic rendering of the turbulent seas and the extremely adept use of contrasts in light.

6

7

The invention of the angel who appears before the sleeping Mark, was doubtless the work of Domenico.

8. Jacopo Robusti, known as 'Tintoretto'
(Venice 1519-1594)

Virgin with Child and Saints Cecilia, Marina, Cosma and Damian

Canvas, 341 × 251 cm
Acquisition: 1812, following the Napoleonic suppressions, (cat. 221)
Latest restoration: 1991-92

This piece was originally on the first altar on the left in the Church of Santi Cosma e Damiano on the island of Giudecca. It dates to the 1550s. The chromatic alteration of the once much lighter large clouds is unfortunately irreversible.

9. Paolo Caliari (Veronese)
(Verona 1528-Venice 1588)

The Marriage of Saint Catherine

Canvas, 377 × 241 cm
Acquisition: 1918, taken back after the First World War from the church of S. Caterina, became State property following the Napoleonic suppressions, (cat. 1324)
Latest restoration: 1986

8

7. Jacopo Robusti, known as 'Tintoretto'
(Venice 1519-1594)
and Domenico Robusti, known as 'Tintoretto'
(Venice 1560-1635)

The Dream of Saint Mark

Canvas, 388 × 314 cm
Acquisition: 1924, from the Church of S. Maria degli Angeli at Murano, (cat. 875)
Latest restoration: 1992-93

A collaborative effort by Jacopo Tintoretto and his son Domenico, originally located at the side of the altar in the chapel of the Chapter Room of the Scuola Grande di San Marco, which Jacopo strove to complete in 1585 in order to for his father and two friends to gain acceptance into the Dominican confraternity.

Painted for the high altar of the Venetian church of Santa Caterina.
The painting was taken from the church during the World War I.
The emphasis is by now pre-Baroque, with its extraordinary chromatic elements and serene beauty of the images.
The piece was very well received by contemporaries and artists of the following century. Dated around 1575, near the time when Veronese painted the canvases for the ceiling of the Sala del Collegio in the Doge's Palace.

10

**10. Paolo Caliari,
known as 'Veronese'**
(Verona 1528-Venice 1588)

Annunciation

Canvas, 271 × 541 cm
Acquisition: 1812, following
the Napoleonic
suppressions, (cat. 260)
Latest restoration: 1969-70

From the Scuola dei
Mercanti, (still intact and the
left of the Church of
Madonna dell'Orto), where
the piece was kept in the
Sala dell'Albergo above the
door. The symbol of the
confraternity – a hand
blessing the cross – can be
seen at the centre under the
drum, while on the pillars of
the middle columns are the
coats of arms of the
commissioners, the
Cadabrazzo and Cottoni
families. The work was
widely praised by
contemporaries. It was
painted in 1578, a date
revealed by reflection
analyses under a thick
repainted layer which,
together with other
alterations (the insertion of a
piece of floor on the lower
central area near the door,
the shortening of the upper
part), greatly influence our
understanding of the piece.
The composition still reveals
some excellent details from
its original luminosity, such
as the vase on the
balustrade, and appears as a
succession and synthesis of
scenic elements, closed at
the background by a small
temple which was perhaps
inspired by the Church of
Santa Maria Nuova in
Vicenza, completed by
Palladio also in 1578.

**11. Titian (Tiziano
Vecellio)**
(Pieve di Cadore c. 1488/90
-Venice 1576)

Pietà

Canvas, 353 × 347 cm
Acquisition: 1814, following
the Napoleonic
suppressions, (cat. 400)
Latest restoration: 1984–85

This work reached the
Accademia from the church
of Sant'Angelo, where it had
been placed in 1631 at the
end of the great plague.
Ridolfi in 1648 recalls how
it had been created by Titian
for the chapel of Cristo at
the Frari in exchange for
being buried there. But the
negotiations failed and the
painting, which was created
from seven different pieces
of canvas, was brought into
the workshop. A document
recently discovered in the
secret Archive of the Vatican
confirms that in March of
1575 the painting was
displayed at the Frari. In
fact, a papal nuncio decree
asks that the image, which

10

11

was placed on an different altar from the one agreed upon, be returned to Titian. In 1576, while the plague was at its worst, Titian had nearly transformed the painting into a large *ex voto* against the epidemic, an exceptional autobiographical statement. As the writing near the bottom attests, the work was definitively completed by Jacopo Palma il Giovane before Titian's death on August 27 of that year: "*Quod Titianus inchoatum reliquit, Palma reventer absolvit deoq dicavit*

opus" ("*that which Titian left unfinished, Palma brought reverently to completion and dedicated the work to God*"). During the most recent restoration project it was revealed how limited Palma's actual intervention was, regarding primarily some touches to camouflage the various grafts of canvas, the angel with the torch painted over a previous putto left unfinished by Titian, and the writing itself. The work is centred largely around the theme of death, eucharistic sacrifice and

resurrection. Like Michelangelo, Titian also portrayed himself in the *Pietà* destined for his grave: the old man lying prostrate in front of the Virgin – probably Nicodemus – is a self-portrait.

12. Paolo Caliari known as 'Veronese'
(Verona 1528–Venice 1588)

Crucifixion

Canvas, 285 cm x 447 cm
Acquisition: 1834, following the Napoleonic suppressions (cat. 255)

Latest restoration: 1969
The freedom of the *Christ in the House of Levi* is replaced here by a strict adhesion to the evangelical text, a sign of a deep change in the political and religious climate in Venice, surely accelerated by the plague of 1575. The dark and dramatic atmosphere of the scenes are typical of Veronese's last phase, to which the painting belongs; it was completed around 1582 and was originally in the church of San Nicolò della Lattuga at the Frari.

Leandro Bassano, Bernardo Strozzi, Giambattista Tiepolo, Luca Giordano, Jacopo Tintoretto, Bonifacio Veronese and Pordenone

Room 11 was reopened in 1946 by Carlo Scarpa after covering it with a thick grey canvas. This was to be a provisional arrangement while a definitive plan was implemented – which was not to be implemented by Scarpa. In the 1980s, this large room was renovated, repeating the motives used by Scarpa in its twin room (Room 10). In 1996, fragments of the ceiling of the Church of the Scalzi painted by Giambattista Tiepolo were placed here using specially created supports for their display.

Giambattista Tiepolo, The Discovery of the True Cross and Saint Elena, *detail*

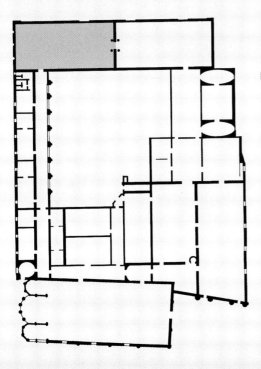

1. Leandro da Ponte, known as 'Bassano'
(Bassano 1557-1622)

Resurrection of Lazarus

Canvas, 416 × 237 cm
Acquisition: 1815,
following the Napoleonic
suppressions, (cat. 252)
Latest restoration: 1981

Returned from Paris in
1815, this altarpiece was
originally on the high
altar of the Mocenigo
house in the church of
Santa Maria della Carità.
Generally believed to be
from the beginning of
the century, the painting
reveals Bassano's dignified
translation of his father's
artistic language.

Bernardo Strozzi
(Genoa 1581-Venice
1644)

2. *Portrait of the Knight
Giovanni Grimani*

Canvas, 225 × 143 cm
Acquisition: 1981, by
purchase, (cat. 1358)
Latest restoration: 1995

Giovanni Grimani, while
he was ambassador in
Vienna from 1636 to
1640, was knighted by
the Emperor. This large
portrait was probably
ordered from Strozzi
upon his return from
Vienna, immediately after
1640. Grimani is
portrayed with the
golden stole, symbol of
knighthood. This work is
a masterpiece from the
height of Strozzi's artistic
maturity. Hints of
Rubens and Van Dyck are
brought together with a
decidedly Venetian
treatment of light and
colour. The great painters
of the 18th century, from
Fra' Galgario to
Alessandro Longhi and
including Giambattista
Tiepolo himself, will
look to this kind of
portraiture for their
official portraits

1

3. *Feast in the House of Simon*

Canvas, 257 × 737 cm
Acquisition: 1911, by
purchase, (cat. 777)
Latest restoration: 1981

This large painting,
purchased in Vicenza in
1911, comes from the
chapel of Palazzo Gorleri
in Genoa. It was probably
originally painted for the
parlour of the Santa
Maria in Passione
monastery in Genoa. In
addition to its attempt to
translate the style of
Caravaggio into a
Baroque setting, the
painting reveals a distinct
Venetian influence, a style
well known to Strozzi
even before he moved to
Venice.

2

11

3

95

Giambattista Tiepolo
(Venice, 1696–Madrid 1770)

4. Punishment of the Serpents

Canvas, 167 × 1355 cm
Acquisition: 1892, following
the Napoleonic
suppressions, (cat. 343)
Latest restoration: 1992

This large frieze was
originally under the choir in
the church of Santi Cosma
e Damiano on the
Giudecca. It was owned by
the state after the
Napoleonic suppressions,
and ended up in the church
of Santa Maria e San
Liberale in Castelfranco
Veneto, where it remained

rolled-up for almost sixty
years. These events damaged
the work, but all its
expressive potential remains
intact; indeed, it is precisely
for this reason that the large
gaps have not been filled in.
Dating to around 1731–32,
the painting depicts the
biblical episode of the
bronze serpent erected by
Moses in the desert in order
to heal the snake bites sent
by God to punish the
people of Israel who had
not shown the proper faith
or patience.

5. Moses and Aaron

Fresco, 335 × 446 × 180 cm
(cat. 1376)

*6. Announcement to the Prophet
Nathan*

Fresco, 335 × 446 × 180 cm
(cat. 1378)

7. David and his Wife Mikal

Fresco, 335 × 446 × 180 cm
(cat. 1377)
Latest restoration: 1995–96

The Scalzi Carmelites
commissioned Tiepolo to
decorate the ceiling of the
church of Santa Maria di
Nazareth, the last of the great
religious cycles on fresco by
the artist. The church was

destroyed by an Austrian
bomb intended for the
nearby railway station on the
night of October 24, 1915.
The contract was stipulated
on September 13, 1743 and
on October 1 Girolamo
Mengozzi, nicknamed
Colonna (column), began to
create the artificial
architectural features for the
sum of 1500 ducats; Tiepolo
would receive 3000 ducats
for his work. He studied the
composition in a
considerable number of
sketches and prepared two
oval drafts on canvas: the
first, probably the one for
which he was paid 100

5

4

zecchini on September 13, 1743, is preserved in the Accademia Gallery (Room 17, cat. 91); the second, which was closest to the final version, is today at the Paul Getty Museum in Malibu. Both painters received payments from April 14 until November 23, 1745, dates which should also correspond to the actual execution of the vast work. On the central part was celebrated the miraculous *Transportation of the Holy House of Nazareth*. In the decoration on the perimeter of the vault were other episodes depicting various parts of the Old Testament foreshadowing Mary herself, or the theme and the Holy House. Another four pendentives, one of which is lost, depicted annunciation scenes. Recovered from the depository where they had been stored after the disaster, they were then transferred onto canvas in 1969. The last part of the work restored the slightly curved shape. On the first, a few condensed episodes from Exodus are represented: Moses, angered by the smelting of the golden calf, breaks the tablets of the law bestowed upon him by God, which will be given to him a second time. Returning from Mount Sinai, his face becomes radiant after having spoken with the Lord and thus he appears to Aaron. On the second, God, in the form of an angel, announces to the prophet Nathan his alliance with David and the permanence of his dynasty, the depository of the messianic promises. On the last one, David responds harshly to his wife Mikal, who had chastised him for humiliating himself by dancing before the ark of the Lord. The extraordinary power of the line, the suggestion of the green tones on the light background and the effective synthesis make these fragments – which are clearly by the artist himself, at least the figurative parts – works of the utmost quality. As documentation also confirms, the backgrounds belong to Mengozzi, while Tiepolo had to unify the whole work with small retouches. His unmistakable luminous brushstrokes are found in many areas on these three pendentives and on the following four loggias.

11

6

7

8

9

10

11

12

Giambattista Tiepolo
(Venice 1696–Madrid 1770)

8. *Worshipers Facing a Loggia*
Fresco, 405 × 216 cm
(cat. 836)

9. *Loggia*
Fresco, 405 × 216 cm
(cat. 1375)

10. *Worshipers Facing a Loggia*
Fresco, 405 × 216 cm
(cat. 837)

11. *Worshipers Facing a Loggia*
Fresco, 405 × 216 cm
(cat. 1374)
Latest restoration: 1995–96

At the four curved corners of the ceiling were some railed galleries which survived the bombing and were recovered between 1916 and 1917. Two of these (cat. 836 and 837) were displayed at the Accademia Galleries in 1919, the other two remained in storage until the most recent restoration. On three of these, Tiepolo painted some praying worshipers, awed spectators of the miracle. The fourth, which is empty, should belong to Colonna, but here as in the other loggias, Tiepolo surely intervened with some corrections in order to render the work more uniform.

12. *Saint Helena and the Discovery of the True Cross*
Canvas, 500 cm diameter
Acquisition: 1812, following the Napoleonic suppressions, (cat. 462)
Latest restoration: 1982

This large ceiling painting was made for the church of Le Cappuccine in Castello, which was destroyed. The painting was surrounded by decorations by Girolamo Mengozzi (Colonna). From about the same time as the first works delivered in 1743 by Tiepolo to the Scuola dei Carmini, it shares with these the marvellous chromatic polyphony and refined 'upside-down' perspective. A sketch showing an early idea for the painting is also on display here (Room 17, cat. 789).

13. **Luca Giordano**
(Naples 1634-1705)

Crucifixion of Saint Peter

Canvas, 195 × 257 cm
Acquisition: 1910, by
purchase, (cat. 751)
Latest restoration: 1984

The signature and the
date are on the painting:
"L. Giordano F. 1692",
but these have been
recognised as false. The
authorship is certain, but
the date is less so, with
critics generally placing
the work – still with
some exceptions –
around 1659-60. The
dramatic component of
the composition evokes
the paintings of
Caravaggio, but the
dilution of the forms into
the colours prefigures a
Rococo style.

13

11

14

Jacopo Robusti
known as 'Tintoretto'
(Venice 1519-1594)

14. *Madonna dei Camerlenghi*

Canvas, 221 × 520cm
Acquisition: 1883, (cat. 210)
Latest restoration: 1992

This large painting, also known as the *Madonna of the Treasurers*, carries an inscription on the lower left: "unanimis concordiae/ simbolus/1566". The work was destined for the Camerlenghi palazzo at Rialto. The Camerlenghi were the financial magistrates of the Venetian Republic. The date of 1566 refers to the offices of Michele Pisani, Lorenzo Dolfin and Marino Malipiero, whose coats of arms are shown on the plinth to the lower left, but the actual execution of the piece occurred when Marino Malipiero's command ended in around 1567, a date which can actually be seen under magnification just below

that of 1566. The horizontal development of the composition, emphasised by the succession of porticoes with the marvellous landscape beyond them, and the penetrating characterisation of the commissioners followed by their secretaries make this work masterpiece of the Venetian votive painting tradition.

15. *Crucifixion*

Canvas, 280 × 444 cm
Acquisition: 1891, from the Scuola del Rosario in the church of Santi Giovanni e Paolo, (cat. 213)
Latest restoration: 1967

Originally in the Scuola del Santissimo Sacramento, in the Venetian church of San Severo, this piece dates to around 1554-55 and reveals a period in which Tintoretto embraced the painting of Paolo Veronese.

16. **Bonifacio de' Pitati known as 'Bonifacio Veronese'**
(Verona 1487–Venice 1553)

Lazarus the Beggar

Canvas, 206 × 438 cm
Acquisition: 1812, by purchase, (cat. 291)
Latest restoration: 1991–92

Purchased from the Grimani family for the Accademia Galleries at the request of the viceroy Eugenio Beauharnais; originally the piece was in the Giustiniani palazzo, where it was still recorded in 1763. Dated around 1543–45, this is considered the artist's masterpiece for his ability to bring together the teachings of both Titian and Tintoretto. The episode depicted here refers to the evangelical parable of Epulone refusing to give alms to poor Lazarus, but here this becomes the pretext for an extraordinary description of Venetian villa life.

17. **Giovanni Antonio de' Sacchis, known as 'Pordenone'**
(Pordenone 1483/84–Ferrara 1539)

The Blessed Lorenzo Giustiniani and Saints

Canvas, 420 × 222 cm
Acquisition: 1815, following the Napoleonic suppressions, (cat. 316)
Latest restoration: 1997

This altarpiece was commissioned from Pordenone in 1532 for 100 ducats, and was for the altar of the Renier family, which is still in the Church of Madonna dell'Orto. Brought to Paris in 1797, it was returned to Venice in 1815 and entrusted to the Accademia Galleries. The figure of Lorenzo Giustiniani – canonised in 1690 – blesses Saints Louis, Francis, Bernard, John the Baptist and two "turchini", who were secular canons from San Giorgio in Alga, to which order the church was entrusted. The articulation of the composition, the elongated modes and twists of the figures, and in particular the pose of the Michelangelesque body of John the Baptist, are all characteristics of mannerism, which was effectively introduced in Veneto by Pordenone himself.

11

16

11

17

Marco Ricci, Giuseppe Zais
and Francesco Zuccarelli

This room is formed by the long end of the Palladio hallway, and its large windows are probably the work of Lazzari in the 19th century. In 1912 three doors and their surmountig ornamental panels were installed. These may have come from a palazzo in Brescia, and were painted by Pietro Scalvini (Brescia, 1718-92) and Saverio Gandini (Cremona, c. 1729–Brescia, 1796). On the door with the depiction of a sculpture is Scalvini's signature and the date, 1778.

Francesco Zuccarelli,
The Abduction of
Europe, *detail*

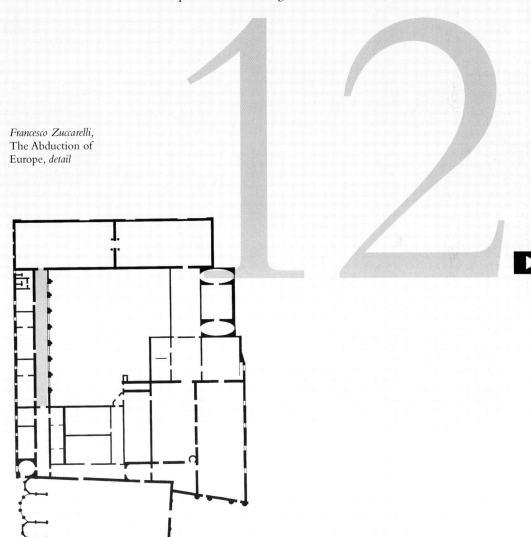

Marco Ricci
(Belluno 1676–Venice
1730)

1. *Landscape with a Stream,
Monks and Washerwomen*

Canvas, 136 × 98 cm
Acquisition: 1878, by
purchase, (cat. 457)
Latest restoration: 1963

2. *Landscape with Horses at
the Trough*

Canvas, 136 × 198 cm
Acquisition: 1878, by
purchase, (cat. 456)
Latest restoration: 1963

These two *pendants* are
recorded in the Corniani
Algarotti gallery in
Treviso.
In the first the Piave
valley is discernable, and
it also seems to appear in
the second, where an old
fountain is also shown.
With its vivid and
attentive realism, the
piece is of fundamental
importance amongst the
output the artist, who
was inspired by the
drawings of Titian and
the engravings of
Domenico Campagnola.
Originally the piece was
thought to be from 1720,
but more recently critics
have correctly dated in
towards 1715.

Giuseppe Zais, attr.
(Canale d'Agordo 1709
-Treviso 1781)

3. *Landscape with Agar
and the Angel*

Canvas, 71 × 94 cm

4. *Landscape with Tobias
and the Angel*

Canvas, 72 cm × 96 cm
Acquisition: 1906, by
purchase, (cat. 721, 722)
Latest restoration: 1984

These two paintings, with
the two biblical stories
immersed in the
landscape – as they also
occur in Fetti's *Parables* –
are traditionally attributed
to Zais, although they
seem closer to the style
of Antonio Diziani.

3

4

12

5

6

108

Giuseppe Zais
(Canale d'Agordo 1709
-Treviso 1781)

5. *Ancient Ruins with a
Large Arch and Columns*

Canvas, 96 × 146 cm
Acquisition: 1923, from
the Palazzo Reale, (cat.
847)

Latest restoration: 1984

6. *Landscape with a Stream
and Dancing Villagers*

Canvas, 96 × 142 cm
Acquisition: 1923, from
the Palazzo Reale (Royal

Palace, (cat. 848)
Latest restoration: 1984

In these landscapes from
the end of the 1730s, the
influence of Marco Ricci
on Zais's work is quite
clear; Zais renders Ricci's
style more elegant, but
keeps it vivid and bright.

7. **Francesco Zuccarelli**
(Pitigliano 1702-Florence
1788/89)

Rape of Europa

Canvas, 143 × 208 cm
Acquisition: 1923, from
the Palazzo Reale,
(cat. 858)

Latest restoration: 1982

On the collar of the dog
at the lower left is the
signature. This canvas, like
its *pendant* with the
Bacchanal (Room 12, cat.
859), was painted for the
Pisani family, who kept it

in their splendid and
regal villa in Stra. It is
considered the artist's
masterpiece, and dates to
around 1740-1750. The
story of the rape of
Europa, taken from
Ovid's *Metamorphoses*, is
rendered with the same
grace and ease as an
Metastasian melodrama.

12

7

8

Giuseppe Zais
(Canale d'Agordo 1709–
Treviso 1781)

8. *Landscape with a River,
Bridge and Flocks*

Canvas, 97 × 142 cm
Acquisition: 1923, from the
Palazzo Reale, (cat. 849)
Latest restoration: 1985

9. *Ruins of a Vaulted Building*

Canvas, 97 × 147 cm
Acquisition: 1923, from the
Palazzo Reale (cat. 846)
Latest restoration: 1984

Marco Ricci's influence on
Zais is also evident in these
paintings from the end of
the 1730s. Zais renders
Ricci's style more elegant,
but keeps it vivid and bright.

Francesco Zuccarelli
(Pitigliano, 1702–Florence,
1788/89)

10. *Landscape with a Lady on
Horseback*

Canvas, transported from
another canvas, 115 × 133 cm
Acquisition: 1923, from the
Palazzo Reale (cat. 861)
Latest restoration: 1984

11. *Landscape with a Boy
Fishing*

Canvas, 116 × 135 cm
Acquisition: 1923, from the
Palazzo Reale (cat. 862)
Latest restoration: 1985

These two landscapes once
belonged to the Pisani
family, and date to around
1740-50. They present with
gentle and festive grace and
fresh colours the pastoral
theme that was so dear to
18th century poetics.

9

10

11

12

Giuseppe Zais
(Canale d'Agordo 1709
-Treviso 1781)

12. *Bacchanal*

Canvas, 142 × 209 cm
Acquisition: 1923, from the
Palazzo Reale, (cat. 859)
Latest restoration: 1982

Pendant of the *Abduction
of Europe* (Room 12, cat.
858), also belonging to
the Pisani family and
painted during the same
period. While fauns and
nymphs dance together in
the idyllic landscape, the
drunk Bacchus rests in
the shade of a rustic hut.

13. *Hunt for the Bull*

Canvas, 114 × 150 cm
Acquisition: 1949, from
the Palazzo Reale,
(cat. 864)
Latest restoration: 1984

Originally in the
Benedictine convent of
San Giorgio Maggiore,
this work is considered to
be from the early period
of the artist's career, a
little after 1732, when he
arrived in Venice. Even
the bloody episode here
of the hunt for the bull is
interpreted with a
pastoral grace, and the
work was widely praised
in artistic centres such as
Paris and London, where
the artist sojourned.

12

13

14

14. **Antonio Diziani**
(Venice 1737-1797)

Landscape with Mary Magdalene

Canvas, 132 × 117 cm
Acquisition: 1807, from the old Accademia, (cat. 455)

This is the painting that Antonio Diziani – the son of the more famous Gaspare – presented in 1766 to gain admittance to the Accademia, into which he was accepted only on 11th September, 1774.

Gaspare Diziani
(Belluno 1689-Venice 1767)

15. *Moses and the Burning Bush*

Canvas, 56 × 96 cm

16. *Moses and the Tablets of the Law*

Canvas, 56 × 96 cm
Acquisition: 1838, following the Napoleonic suppressions, (cat. 459, 460)
Latest restoration: 1980

These two *pendants* are largely considered to have been painted in collaboration with the artist's son Antonio, who worked on the landscape.

15

17. **Francesco Zuccarelli**
(Pitigliano 1702–Florence
1788–89)

*Landscape with a Resting
Hunter*

Canvas, 79 × 97 cm
Acquisition: 1959, from
the Palazzo Reale,
(cat. 1333)
Latest restoration: 1993

Originally perhaps in the
convent of San Giorgio
Maggiore, this painting –
of which there is a copy
on the antiquities market
– dates to around the
1740s. The typical idyllic
representation of nature is
strong in the group with
the resting hunter, the
horse and the two dogs,
rendered with an unusual
naturalness. This aspect
reveals Zuccarelli's
familiarity with Dutch
landscape artists such as
Berchem and
Wouwermann.

17

12

16

Jacopo Bassano and portraits by Jacopo Tintoretto

Obtained by the merging of three cells of the Carità convent. With the first restructuring work the ceiling of the first area, which had previously been under a large canvas, was revealed, showing the decoration by Tranquillo Orsi. The remodelling was performed by Carlo Scarpa in 1947.

Jacopo Bassano,
Adoration of the
Shepherds, *detail*

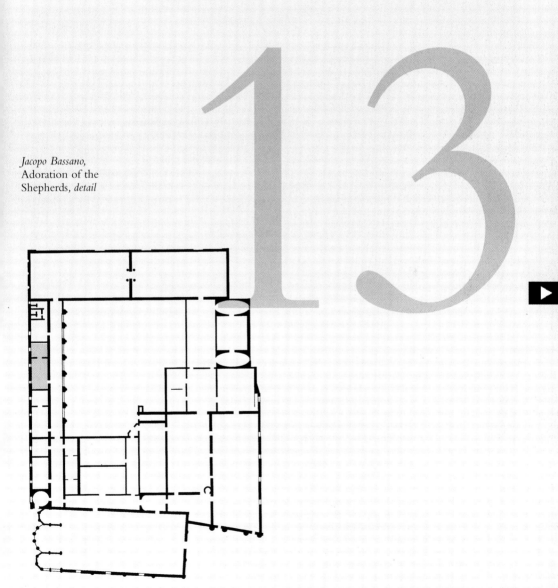

1

3

1. Jacopo da Ponte, known as 'Bassano', and his workshop
(Bassano 1517-1592)

Landscape with Shepherd and the Burning Bush

Canvas, 45 × 114 cm
Acquisition: 1838, donation from Girolamo Contarini, (cat. 415)
Latest restoration: 1963

Originally attributed to Jacopo, today it is believed to have come from his workshop, perhaps derived from models by Francesco Bassano.

Jacopo da Ponte, known as 'Bassano'
(Bassano 1517-1592)

2. *Adoration of the Shepherds*

Canvas, 95 × 140cm
Acquisition: 1983, by purchase, (cat. 1360)

This may be the painting identified in 1620 in the Giusti del Giardino collection, indeed, the piece was purchased from Count Justo Giusti himself. Nonetheless, Ridolfi also makes mention in 1648 of the existence of a very similar work in the house of Cristoforo Orsetti, in which Bassano was believed to imitate "the elegance of Padovanino". In this composition, which evokes Titian-like themes, there is a unique blend of Parmigianino influences (most evident in the image of the Virgin), mannerist refinement and naturalistic observations in the depiction of the animals and the faces of the shepherds. It dates to 1545 or shortly after.

3. *Rest in Egypt*

Canvas, 52 × 102 cm
Acquisition: 1838, donation from Girolamo Contarini, (cat. 410)

The main group of the Madonna with the two children is found in other works by Bassano. The painting recalls a composition described by Ridolfi (1648) in the house of the artist's great-grandson at Bassano.

13

2

4

**Jacopo Robusti,
known as 'Tintoretto'**
(Venice 1519-1594)

*4. Portrait of the Procurator
Antonio Cappello*

Canvas, 114 × 80 cm
Acquisition: 1812,
following the Napoleonic
suppressions, (cat. 236)
Latest restoration: 1993-94

The identification of the
portrait rests on a now
lost 19th century
document. The portrait is
of Antonio Cappello,
from the San Polo area of
Venice and born probably
in 1494.
He carried out many
demanding tasks –
including that of
Procurator in 1525 – for

the Republic until his
death in 1565. The
portrait is from the
Procuratia de' Supra (the
office in Saint Mark's
Square of the procurators
concerned primarily with
the Basilica and its
treasures), where sources
record its presence, even
attributing it to Titian.
The *ante quem* date for
the piece is 1565, when
Cappello died. Indeed,
the work is similar to
other official portraits
painted in the early 1560s
which also bear the mark
of Titian's influence.

5. Portrait of Battista Morosini

Canvas, 96 × 57 cm
Acquisition: 1838, by
donation from Girolamo
Contarini, (cat. 237)
Latest restoration: 1993-94

The identification of the
subject is based on the
Tintoretto-inspired
portrait in the Doge's
Palace, where Battista
Morosini appears older,
and by this time is
Procurator. The son of
Francesco, Battista was
born in 1537 and died in
1598. The painting appears
to be the product of
polished routine, but also
reveals a studied effort
from the artist. It dates to
before 1573.

**6. Andrea Michieli,
known as 'Vicentino'**
(Vicenza 1542-1617)

Paradise

Canvas, 116 × 86 cm
Acquisition: 1978, by
purchase, (cat. 1354)

This is the first preparatory
study for the *Paradise* in the
Basilica dei Frari, and dates
to the beginning of the 17th
century. Another study can
be found in the Walker Art
Gallery in Liverpool. The
influence of Tintoretto –
the 16th century artist most
imitated by Venetian late-
mannerists, of whom
Vicentino is a good
example – in this
composition is quite
evident.

5

6

7. Jacopo Negretti, known as 'Palma il Giovane'
(Venice 1548-1628)

The Crucifixion of Saint Peter

Canvas, 168 × 132 cm
Acquisition: 1901,
donation from M.
Guggenheim, (cat. 660)
Latest restoration: 1963

Probably an early idea for a ceiling work, which is today unknown or perhaps was never constructed. On the upper part, with the Trinity and the Virgin at the centre surrounded by angels and the symbols of the Passion, and on the lower portion with the blessed, including Adam and Eve, the artist imitates a signed composition which is in a private collection in Rome. The crucifixion scene seems to betray a continuing influence of the Michelangelo fresco in the Paolina Chapel. The work dates to about 1614.

8. Domenico Robusti, known as 'Tintoretto'
(Venice 1560-1635)

Portrait of a Contarini Procurator

Canvas, 117 × 87 cm
Acquisition: 1919,
following the Napoleonic
suppressions, (cat. 1012)
Latest restoration: 1993

The painting was originally in the Procuratia de Citra (the office in Saint Mark's Square for the Procurators of the Basilica who dealt with its holdings on 'this side' – 'de Citra' – of the Grand Canal), and carries the Contarini coat of arms and the initials L.C. at the lower left. The work is probably a portrait of Giovanni Paolo Contarini, who was elected Procurator in 1594 and died in 1604.

9. Jacopo da Ponte, known as 'Bassano'
(Bassano 1517-1592)

Saint Eleutherius Blesses the Devotees

Canvas, 280 × 174 cm
Acquisition: 1829,
following the Napoleonic
suppressions (cat. 401)
Latest restoration: 1993

Originally on the high altar of the church of Sant'Eleuterio in Vicenza, belonging to the Marzari confraternity. Recently critics have dated the work at 1565. It is probably a collaboration with the artist's son Francesco – perhaps a depiction of the young man in prayer – which must have begun even at the planning stage, and is especially evident in the weak Christ amongst the clouds.

8

13

7

13

12

10. Jacopo Robusti known as 'Tintoretto'
(Venice 1519-1594)

The Procurator Andrea Cappello

Canvas, 115 × 86 cm
Acquisition: 1812,
following the Napoleonic
suppressions, (cat. 234)
Latest restoration: 1994

Originally in the
Procuratia de Supra, this
piece is probably the one
indicated in 1812 by
Pietro Edwards (the first
curator of the Accademia
Galleries) as the *Portrait of
a Veneto Senator* by Jacopo
Tintoretto. On the right
are the Cappello coat of

arms and the initial "A".
The subject is indeed
Andrea Cappello, son of
Silvano, who was elected
procurator in 1537 and
died in 1564, the *ante
quem* date for the
completion of the portrait,
which was obviously
painted from life.

11. Jacopo da Ponte known as Bassano
(Bassano 1517-1592)

Saint Jerome

Canvas, 119 × 154 cm
Acquisition: 1900, by
purchase, (cat. 652)

Dating to the beginning
of the 1560s, this is

almost certainly the same painting seen by Ridolfi (1648) in the Widmann house. It is unanimously recognised as one of the artist's masterpieces, revealing a great sense of monumentality. The artist has one eye on the German figurative tradition and the other on the harmony between hermit and nature, a characteristic of Giovanni Bellini. He also adds a decidedly modern psychological aspect: the reluctance of Jerome to continue striking himself. Indeed, the saint holds the stone stained with blood almost hidden behind his back while he ponders the sacrifice of the cross. He is surrounded by the usual attributes, which are fine still-lifes in their own right.

12. **Titian (Tiziano Vecellio)**
(Pieve di Cadore c. 1480-90-Venice 1576)
Virgin with Child

Canvas, 124 × 96 cm
Acquisition: 1981, bequest from the will of Leonardo Albertini, (cat. 1359)

For private devotion, this painting belonged to the Matenza Marquises of Milan, at least from 1616 until 1879, when it passed to the Pinetti Martinengo family of Bergamo. It was purchased in 1916 by Luigi Albertini, father of Leonardo. To the left of the composition can be seen the burning bush, symbol of the eternal virginity of Mary. X-rays have revealed that the artist used a canvas for this painting on which he had previously painted a praying saint. From about 1560.

10

13

11

13

13

14

Jacopo Robusti, known as 'Tintoretto'

(Venice 1519-1594)

13. *Salomon and the Queen of Saba*

Canvas, 122 × 127 cm
Acquisition: 1988, with the recoveries by Rodolfo Sivieri, (cat. 1381)

This painting was originally in a private collection in Bologna, then in the Simotti Rocchi collection in Rome; it was finally recovered in Germany in 1954 by Rodolfo Siviero. The painting is part of a series of allegorical subjects taken from episodes the Old and New Testaments, which have been attributed to Tintoretto's early phase, when he was closest to Andrea Schiavone, around 1545.

14. *The Procurator Jacopo Soranzo*

Canvas, 106 × 90 cm
Acquisition: 1812, following the Napoleonic suppressions, (cat. 245)
Latest restoration: 1957

Painted for the Procuratoria de Supra, this work was originally in the form of a lunette, and to make it rectangular it was joined at the top – on the left with a triangular piece of canvas and on the right with a short strip to frame Soranzo. The alteration probably took place at the end of the 1500s, when many paintings were adapted by Tintoretto and his son Domenico for the new rooms of the rebuilt Procurators' Offices. The fragmentary writing carries the name of the subject and the date of 1522, which indicates when Soranzo took office and not when the painting was completed. The portrait dates to around 1550, just after the portrait of Soranzo with a group of relatives, today at the Castello Sforzesco in Milan. Both paintings are from before 1551, however, the year the Procurator died. Despite its official "formal" use, the picture reveals a surprising expressive power.

16

15. *Portrait of Doge Alvise Mocenigo*

Canvas, 116 × 97 cm
Acquisition: 1817, following the Napoleonic suppressions, (cat. 233)
Latest restoration: 1993

From the Procuratoria de Ultra, the office in Saint Mark's Square of the Procurators who dealt with the Basilica's holdings on the other side – Ultra – of the Grand Canal. As with the preceding portrait, this one was originally in the form of a lunette, and depicts Alvise Mocenigo, who was born in 1507 and served as Doge from 1570 until 1577, the year the portrait was made, probably just after the election. In the noble pose and sober tonality can be seen the influence of the style of portraiture practised by Titian, whom Tintoretto had succeeded as the official portrait artist of the Signoria.

16. **Veneto School of the 16ᵗʰ Century**

Allegory of Nature

Panel, 42 × 74 cm
Acquisition: during the 19ᵗʰ century, from the Palazzo Reale (cat. 901)
Latest restoration: 1960

This panel, which shows the *Allegory of Nature*

15

between *Time* and *Truth*, is recorded as having been in the Zecca (mint) in 1788, and passed to Palazzo Reale at the beginning of the 19ᵗʰ century. Previously it was attributed to Andrea Meldolla, known as 'Schiavone' (Zadar, 1522–Venice, 1563), but later it was thought to be from the studio of Bonifacio de' Pitati, known as 'Bonifacio Veronese' (Verona, 1487-Venice, 1553).

17. **Lambert Sustris**
(Amsterdam, around 1515-Venice, after 1591?)

Christ Bound, and a View of Jerusalem

Panel, 63 × 80 cm
Acquisition: 1816, bequest from Girolamo Molin, (cat. 268)
Latest restoration: 1959

The painting came to the Galleries when it was attributed to Schiavone, but the panel is now recognised as the work of Sutris, who often painted scenes of Jerusalem taken from models by the Sutris' first master, Jan van Scorel.

13

17

17th Century Paintings

This room has undergone the same renovations as Room 13.

14

Domenico Fetti, David
with Goliath's head,
detail

3. **Pierfrancesco Mola**
(Coldrerio 1612-1666)

Allegory of the Phlegmatic Temperament

Canvas, 76 × 114 cm
Acquisition: 1955, by purchase, (cat. 1314)
Latest restoration: 1962

This painting was inspired by Carlo Ripa's *Iconologia* (Padua, 1630), in which the relationship between the four elements and human temperament is established: "the choleric for fire", "the sanguine for air", "the melancholy for earth", and "the phlegmatic for water". The figure of the sleeping man represents the "phlegmatic/water" element. As the fountain indicates, the early study of Guercino's work is enriched by exposure to Veneto artistic culture. The work dates to around the middle of the century.

14

1. **Annibale Carracci**
(Bologna 1560-1609)

Saint Francis

Canvas, 91 × 73 cm
Acquisition: 1901, by purchase, (cat. 1189)
Latest restoration: 1955

An early work from around 1585-1586, this painting – of which there are copies in the Galleria Nazionale in Rome and in the Liechtenstein collection in Vaduz – reflects in its great elegance the influence of the major Veneto painters of the 1500s. The landscape is marvellous, with its symbolic elements which are equally valid as still lifes in their own right.

2. **Bernardo Strozzi**
(Genova 1581/82 -Venice 1644)

San Jerome

Canvas, 56 × 47 cm
Acquisition: 1838, by donation from Girolamo Contarini, (cat. 424)
Latest restoration: 1962

This devotional painting of a theme repeated many times by the artist is generally attributed to the early period of Strozzi's stay in Venice, around the 1640s.

3

4. **Domenico Fetti**
(Rome? 1588/89-Venice 1623)

Parable of the Good Samaritan

Canvas, 61 × 45 cm
Acquisition: 1838, by donation from Girolamo Contarini, (cat. 503)
Latest restoration: 1948

"Parables" are among the most common subjects treated by Fetti, such as this one of the good Samaritan. Like its preparatory drawing at the Louvre (inv. 3069), this work dates to about 1617. There are various replicas of the subject, including the one in Gemäldegalerie Dresden, which depicts the subject in a horizontal format.

14

4

5

5. Johann Liss
(Holstein c. 1597–Verona
1631)

Apollo and Marsyas

Canvas, 58 × 48 cm
Acquisition: 1838, by
donation from Girolamo
Contarini, (cat. 674)

Among the last works by
the painter, incorporating
his experience in Venice
with his earlier training
in Rome from the Dutch
admirers of Caravaggio.

6. Domenico Fetti copy
from (Rome? 1588/89–
Venezia 1623)

Portrait of Francesco Andreini

Canvas, 102 × 79 cm
Acquisition: 1838,
donation from Girolamo
Contarini, (cat. 678)
Latest restoration: 1956

A copy of the portrait of
the actor Francesco
Andreini (Pistoia, c.
1548–Mantua, 1624) kept
at the Hermitage in Saint
Petersburg. This painting
mimics 16th century
Venetian or Carpaccio-
inspired models, and dates
to before 1620, when
Andreini left Mantua and
headed first for Milan,
then to France, returning
only after the sudden
departure of Fetti. The
painting depicts the
subject with a mask in his
hand, symbol of his
profession, and uniquely
recalls Eduardo De
Filippo, thereby obtaining
further depth, depicting
not only Francesco
Andreini but every actor,
beyond every limit of
time.

Johann Liss
(Holstein c. 1597–Verona
1631)

7. *The Sacrifice of Isaac*

Canvas, 66 × 85 cm
Acquisition: 1932, by
purchase, (cat. 914)
Latest restoration: 1959

8. *Abel Mourned by his Parents*

Canvas, 68 × 89 cm
Acquisition: 1932, by
purchase, (cat. 913)
Latest restoration: 1959

This painting, along with
the previous one of
which it is a *pendant*, was
purchased from the
Giovanelli collection.
Both paintings date to
the years when the artist
sojourned in Venice
(1624-29). The dramatic
effect of the subject is
diluted in a powerful
melancholy, a result of
the emphasis given to the
landscape where the
event is taking place. *The
Sacrifice* is one of Liss'
masterpieces; there are
other versions of the
second painting, with
variations.

6

7

14

8

9

10

11

9. Tiberio Tinelli
(Venice 1586-1638)

Portrait of Luigi Molin

Canvas, 133 × 115 cm
Acquisition: 1816,
bequest from Girolamo
Molin, (cat. 544)
Latest restoration: 1962

The attribution to Tinelli
– like the identification
of the subject – have by
now been widely
accepted. According to
Ridolfi (1648), Molin
was sent to Mantua by
the Venetian Republic in
1637 for the election of
the new Duke, Carlo II,
and brought Tinelli with
him. The gentleman rests
on a book which, with its
Ducal seal, could well be
the "Commissione
Ducale", containing
instructions for running
the Republic. The busts
in the background in this
case could allude to his
passion for collecting art.

**10. Anonymous,
17th Century**

*Portrait of Procurator
Domenico Contarini*

Canvas, 163 × 102 cm
Acquisition: 1988, with
the recoveries by Rodolfo
Sivieri, (cat. 1382)
Latest restoration: 1988

Recorded in 1927 in the
Giovanelli collection at
San Felice, the piece was
taken by the Nazis and
recovered by Rodolfo
Siviero. It has been
attributed to Nicolas
Regnier, from a time
when his style was
particularly similar to that
of his son-in-law Daniel
van der Dyck. Tiberio
Tinelli has also been
mentioned but after
careful scrutiny of the
best Venetian official
portraits by artists from
Bombelli to Strozzi, the
work's author remains
difficult to identify, in
spite of its obvious
quality.

11. **Bernardo Strozzi**
(Genova 1581/82
-Venice 1644)

Doge Francesco Erizzo

Canvas, 133 × 108 cm
Acquisition: 1920,
by purchase, (cat. 829)
Latest restoration: 1995

The portrait of Francesco
Erizzo – "Del Prete
Genovese" ("By the
Genovese Priest"),
as is stated in two old
inscriptions on the back
of the original canvas –
was originally in the
Erizzo family villa in
Bassano. The family
commissioned the work
from Strozzi, and it was
to be for private
enjoyment; a replica –
which was the official
portrait in the Doge's
Palace – exists in the
Kuntshistorisches
Museum in Vienna.
Erizzo became Doge in
1631 at the age of 65,
and held the title until his
death in 1646. It is
probable, then, given the
apparent age of the
subject, that the portrait
was made immediately
after his election. It is
probably one of the first
portraits painted in
Venice. Reflectographic

analyses have revealed a
conspicuous correction
on the right hand, and
also confirmed the actual
authorship.

12. **Mattia Preti**
(Taverna 1613-1699)

Homer

Canvas, 102 × 81 cm
Acquisition: 1821,
by purchase, (cat. 59)
Latest restoration: 1963

When this piece came to
the Accademia it was
believed to be a work by
Caravaggio; later it was
attributed to
Pierfrancesco Mola, but
today it is unanimously
attributed to the early
years of Mattia Preti.

13. **Anonymous,
17th Century**

A Girl Reading

Canvas, 74 × 69 cm
Acquisition: 1838,
donation from Girolamo
Contarini, (cat. 518)
Latest restoration: 1961

Originally attributed to
Domenico Fetti, the
piece is notable for the
naturalness of the girl
absorbed in her reading.

14. An imitator of
Giambattista Langetti
(Genova 1625-Venezia
1676)

Isaac and Jacob

Canvas, 101 × 75 cm
Acquisition: 1838,
donation from Girolamo
Contarini, (cat. 675)

Previously considered to

be the work of
Domenico Fetti; it has
now been correctly
attributed to Langetti's
circle.

12

14

13

14

Domenico Fetti
(Rome? 1588/89-Venice 1623)

15. *David*

Canvas, 175 × 128 cm
Acquisition: 1838, donation from Girolamo Contarini, (cat. 669)
Latest restoration: 1996

The painting came to the Galleries from a descendent of Giorgio Contarini dagli Scrigni, a patron of Fetti in Venice. It dates from between 1617 and 1619, prior to when the artist resided in Venice. The young man, with his indolent beauty and contemporary dress, harks to Caravaggio's elegant knights in *Buona Ventura* (Lucky Fate) or *The Martyrdom of Saint Matthew*. The face bears some similarity to the one used for the *David* in Dresden (Gemäldegalerie) and in Moscow (Pushkin Museum).

16. *Meditation*

Canvas, 179 × 140cm
Acquisition: 1838, donation from Girolamo Contarini, (cat. 671)
Latest restoration: 1961

Although the donator was a descendent of Giorgio Contarini dagli Scrigni, a

15

patron of Fetti in Venice, this famous painting is believed to have been completed around 1618, before the artist actually resided in Venice. The good fortune of the piece is evidenced by the numerous copies and replicas. There were also some illustrious antecedents such as Dürer's famous engraving, *Melancholy* (1514), or the *Vision of Saint Helena* by Paolo Veronese, or the *Magdalene* by Correggio. In spite of the traditional title, it is likely that the artist kept in mind a part of the second Letter of Paul in the Corinthians 2 (7, 10), which holds that Christian "sadness" that produces repentance leads to salvation, while worldly "sadness" brings on death. The female figure is situated between the still life of the lower part of the painting alluding to death and the "sadness of the world". The grapevine above symbolises life and salvation.

14

education in Tuscany, offers here a free and imaginative interpretation of the subject at the end of the 1640s.

Francesco Maffei
(Vicenza, c. 1605–Padua, 1660)

18. *Mythological Scene*

Canvas, 130 × 160 cm
Acquisition: 1968 by purchase, (cat. 1341)
Latest restoration: 1968

19. *Perseus Beheading Medusa*

Canvas, 130 × 160 cm
Acquisition: 1968 by purchase, (cat. 1340)
Latest restoration: 1968

These two *pendants*, one inspired by Ovid's *Metamorphoses* and the other depicting perhaps Circes and Ulysses, were kept in Budapest until the beginning of this century and ended up in an American collection. They date to 1660, and show the free and whimsical imagination of Maffei, who was raised on the innovative pictorial work of Fetti, Liss and Strozzi.

17

18

17. **Sebastiano Mazzoni**
(Florence? 1611-Venice 1678)

The Annunciation

Canvas, 154 × 112 cm
Acquisition: 1945, from the domanial church of Santa Caterina, (cat. 329)
Latest restoration: 1956

Documented in the church of Santa Caterina, Venice, at the beginning of the nineteenth century, the painting should perhaps be identified with the *Annunciation*, documented in the church of San Luca dal Boschini in 1664. Mazzoni, who had received his early artistic

14

**20. Pietro Muttoni,
known as
'della Vecchia'**
(Venice, 1603-Venice,
1678)

Votive Painting

Canvas, 285 × 227 cm
Acquisition: beginning of
the 19th century, following
the Napoleonic
suppressions, (cat. 868)
Latest restoration: 1961

At the lower centre the
words "ex voto" and at
the right the initials of
the author and the date

1640. The work alludes
perhaps to a religious
conversion. In the sky to
the left appears Saint
Giustina, whose church
originally housed the
work; in the foreground
is a lady adorned with
jewels, seated at the top
of some stairs. An angel
shows her a skull, a
symbol of the transience
of life; at the sides are
Saint Joseph and Saint
John the Evangelist. The
vibrancy of the palette
and the unique invention

are characteristics of
Muttoni's work. He was
called 'della Vecchia' for
his ability to restore and
imitate the 'old' Venetian
masters, Giorgione and
Titian in particular.

14

20

21

21. Giulio Carpioni
(Venezia? 1613-Vicenza
1679)

Crucifixion

Canvas, 205 × 131 cm
Acquisition: 1967, following
the Napoleonic
suppressions, (cat. 1339)
Latest restoration: 1968

This work was originally in
the Church of Santa Lucia
in Udine, and may belong
to the first period of the
artist's stay in Vicenza.
Carpioni reacted against the
late-mannerism conformity
by painting very rigorous
forms, presenting accents of
plasticism and naturalism as
in some of the figures at the
foot of the cross.

19

Giovanni Antonio Pellegrini, Giambattista Tiepolo and Giannantonio Guardi

This is the final part of the long Palladio corridor. The "cell" structure (Rooms 16 and 16a) is to the left, while towards the centre of the building is a large exhibition space that was created from joining three rooms (Room 17); a door remains into one of these rooms. At the end of the room, through the large doorway, is found the famous "oval" stairway designed by Palladio in 1561.

Giannantonio Guardi,
Herminia and Vaprinus
Happen upon the
Wounded Tancredi,
detail

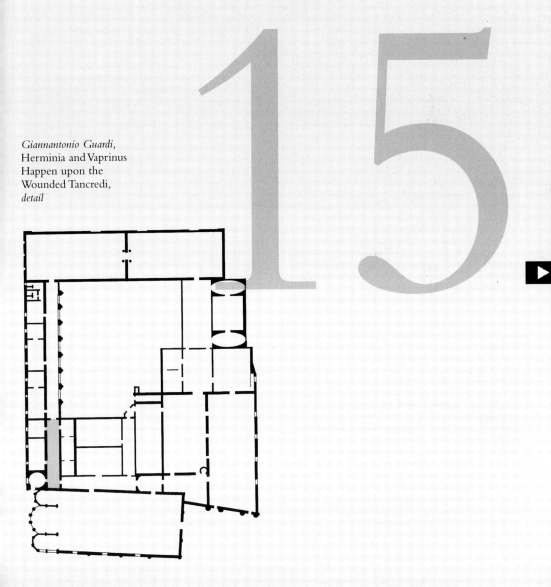

1

4

2

3

1. Giambattista Tiepolo
(Venice, 1696–Madrid, 1770)

Apparition of the Sacred Family to Saint Gaetanus

Canvas, 128 × 73 cm
Acquisition: 1887, by purchase, (cat. 481)
Latest restoration: 1970

Originally painted for the altar of the small chapel of Palazzo Labia in Venice. The sacred image here is conceived in a new way, outside a classical building.
Dates to 1735–36.

Francesco Solimena
(Nocera dei Pagani 1657-Barra 1747)

2. Jacob and Rachel

Canvas, 198 × 150 cm

3. Rebecca and the Servant of Abraham

Canvas, 202 × 150 cm
Acquisition: 1920, by purchase, (cat. 871, 870)
Latest restoration: 1963-64

These two paintings were completed around 1710 for the Venetian home of the Baglioni family on Rio Marin, and were then transferred, towards middle of that century, to the Palazzo Muti in San Cassiano, where they remained until their purchase in 1920. The modelling of the forms and vigorous chiaroscuro contrasts were surely noted by artists such as Giambattista Piazzetta and Giambattista Tiepolo during their early activity.

4. Giambattista Tiepolo
(Venice 1696-Madrid 1770)

Saint Joseph with the Baby Jesus and Saints Francis of Paola, Anne, Anthony and Peter of Alcantara

Canvas, 210 × 114 cm
Acquisition: 1838, following the Napoleonic suppressions, (cat. 484)
Latest restoration: 1960-61

This work was completed in the early 1740s for the church of the Benedictine monks of San Prosdocimo in Padua. It reveals the continuing influence of Piazzetta in the brownish intonation of the colour, and in the compositional structure.

5. Giambattista Pittoni
(Venice 1687-1767)

Annunciation

Canvas, 153 x 205 cm
Acquisition: 1807, from the old Accademia, (cat. 438)
Latest restoration: 1961

Painted in 1757 and displayed in 1777 at the Fiera della Sensa, after the death of the artist.
The work was painted for the Assembly Hall of the Accademia, in its old location at the Fonteghetto della Farina. Angeli and Marinetti also assisted with the decoration of the hall. Pittoni's emphasis seems to have been concentrated on the forms in the composition, which reveal notable stylistic virtuosity.

15

5

6

7

8

6. Giannantonio Guardi
(Vienna 1699-Venice 1760)

Herminia and Vaprinus Happen upon the Wounded Tancredi after his Duel with Argante

Canvas, 250 × 261 cm
Acquisition: 1988, with the recoveries by Rodolfo Sivieri, (cat. 1387)

This work, recovered by Rodolfo Siviero from an English collection, is the only work by Guardi at the Accademia, and was probably part of a cycle of 13 paintings originally in a villa in Este. These works were inspired by an edition of Tasso's *Jerusalem Delivered* with engravings by Piazzetta, and are from around 1750-1755, the height of Guardi's maturity. The paintings are now dispersed among various museums and collections abroad. The painting depicts a scene from the 19th canto of the epic poem and bears a close relation to the Piazzetta drawing at the Biblioteca Reale in Turin and its related engraving. Giannantonio's interpretation incorporates a fresh chromatic scheme, with light brush strokes, while a theatrical flair accentuates the typically Rococo musicality and easy grace of the composition.

Giovanni Antonio Pellegrini
(Venice 1675-1741)

7. The Sculpture

Canvas, 142 × 132 cm

8. The Painting

Canvas, 142 × 132 cm
Acquisition: 1959, by purchase, (cat. 1320, 1319)
Latest restoration: 1959

These two *pendants* from the late 1720s depict the allegory of Painting and Sculpture. They are representative of Pellegrini's subtle elegance and refined use of colour, the artist being one of the protagonists of the international Rococo, the brother-in-law of Rosalba Carriera.

9

9. Angelo Trevisani
(Treviso? 1669-1753/55)

The Expulsion of the Merchants from the Temple

Canvas, 121 × 201 cm
Acquisition: 1912, by purchase, (cat. 790)
Latest restoration: 1960

This is the draft, with notable variations, of the large painting made by the artist in 1732 for the Venetian church of Santi Cosma e Damiano on island of the Giudecca. After the suppressions, it was transferred to Milan, and from 1818 it was kept in the parish church of Somaglia (Lodi, Milan).

10. Giandomenico Tiepolo
(Venice 1727-1804)

Abraham and the Angels

Canvas, 200 × 281 cm
Acquisition: 1807, following the Napoleonic suppressions, (cat. 834)
Latest restoration: 1960

This is the last painting commissioned by the Scuola della Carità to complete the decoration of the new Chancellery which was erected in 1764. A contest was held for this purpose, with entrants sending drafts to a Roman academic commission which included Raffaele Mengs. Giandomenico won the competition, and on March 8, 1773 he began the work for a total of 116 *zecchini* (sequins). A drawing by Giambattista at the State Museum of Berlin appears to have been a counterpart of this piece. The group of angels recalls one painted by his father of the same subject in the Prado, while the figure of Abraham is inspired by the painting in the Luna-Villahermosa collection in Madrid. There are three preparatory studies for Abraham by Giandomenico at the Museo Correr. The smoothness of the colour and the cold purity of the drawing are early reflections of neo-classical thought.

10

Early Works by Giambattista Tiepolo and Sebastiano Ricci

This room has the same original dimensions of the convent cell. It was remodelled by Carlo Scarpa in 1947. Later, in 1959, he also designed the support for Piazzetta's *Fortune Teller.*

Giambattista Tiepolo,
Diana and Acteon, *detail*

Sebastiano Ricci
(Belluno 1640-Venice 1734)

1. *Diana and Calypso*

Canvas, 64 × 76 cm
Acquisition: 1988, with the recoveries by Rodolfo Sivieri, (cat. 1383)

This work was originally in a private British collection, and later to the Contini Bonacossi collection in Florence. It was purchased in 1941 by Goering, who took it to Germany from where it was recovered by Rodolfo Siviero in 1948. Inspired by Ovid's *Metamorphoses*, this painting depicts the moment when Diana points at Calypso, who was guilty of having been seduced by Jove. Appearing

1

almost neo-classical, this composition was also sketched on a sheet of paper which is kept in the Galleries. With its elegant use of colour, the work is attributed to the English period of the artist's career, from 1712-1716.

2. *Bacchanal in Honour of Pan*

Canvas, 84 × 100 cm
Acquisition: 1988, with the recoveries by Rodolfo Sivieri, (cat. 1384)

This painting, previously in the Detsy collection, passed over to the Voss collection of Wiesbaden and then to the Barsanti's in Rome. It was later exported to Germany, where it was recovered by Rodolfo Siviero in 1954. Studied in numerous drawings kept in the royal collections of Windsor and the Accademia Galleries, the piece dates to 1716, after Ricci's brief stay in Paris while returning from London. The circular movement visible in this painting conveys the drunkenness of the bacchanal in honour of Pan, the deity with the horns and the goat's hooves, lover of dance, music and wine.

Giambattista Tiepolo
(Venice 1696-Madrid 1770)

3. *Rape of Europa*

Canvas, 100 × 135 cm
Acquisition: 1898, by purchase, (cat. 435)
Latest restoration: 1993

3

4

16

2

Hera into a bear. Later her son will find her and almost kill her, but Zeus intervenes, changing both into constellations. The four paintings – identical in format and style – are all inspired by Ovid's *Metamorphoses*. Acquired a few years apart in Belluno, the pieces were part of a decorative series, probably in a Belluno palazzo. They are early works by the artist, from around 1720–1721, when Tiepolo was about to abandon dark and dramatic tones and lighten his palette, demonstrating a new ability to articulate figures within space.

4. *Diana and Acteon*

Canvas, 100 cm x 135 cm
Acquisition: 1898,
by purchase, (cat. 440)
Latest restoration: 1993

5. *Apollo and Marsyas*

Canvas, 100 × 135 cm
Acquisition: 1907,
by purchase, (cat. 711)
Latest restoration: 1993

6. *Diana Discovers Calypso Pregnant*

Canvas, 100 × 135 cm
Acquisition: 1907,
by purchase, (cat. 712)
Latest restoration: 1993

On the first canvas is depicted Europa, the daughter of the Phoenician king Agenor, who was taken to Crete by Jove disguised as a bull, where she gave birth to Minos. On the second canvas is Acteon, who is changed a stag after seeing Diana bathing nude; he is then torn to pieces by his own hunting dogs. On the third canvas is the satyr Marsyas, who challenges Apollo with his flute, but Apollo plays his kithara and beats Marsyas, who is then skinned alive and changed into a river as punishment. On the last painting Diana discovers that the huntress Callisto has been seduced by Zeus. Chased away by Diana, she then gives birth to Arcas and is changed by

5

16

6

147

Alessandro Longhi, Giambattista Piazzetta and Fra' Galgario

This room, like the previous Room 16, maintains the same original dimensions of the convent cell. Both rooms were remodelled by Carlo Scarpa in 1947.

Giambattista Piazzetta,
The Fortune Teller,
detail

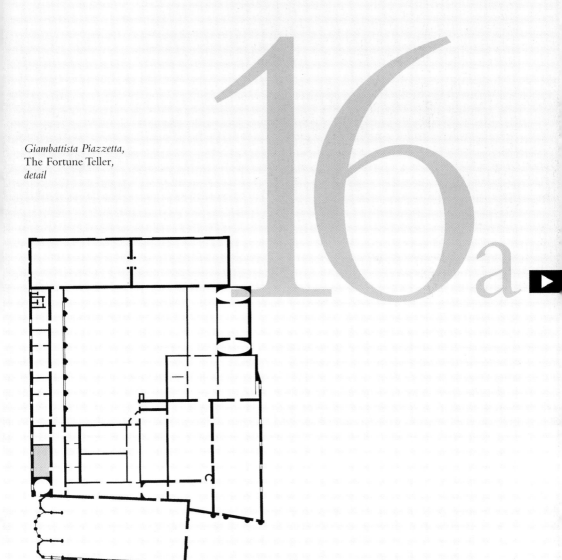

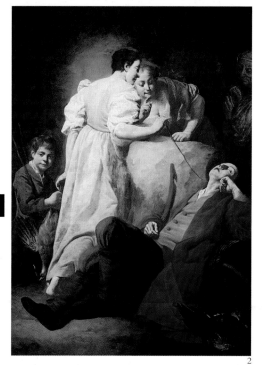

Piazzetta inspired painting. There is a preparatory sketch which carries a dedication and the date of 1745, also the year in which the painting here can be placed.

3. Giambattista Piazzetta
(Venice 1683-1754)

The Fortune Teller

Canvas, 154 × 115 cm
Acquisition: 1887, (cat. 483)
Latest restoration: 1983

Acquired from the merchant Ehrenfreund, on the back of the original canvas there was a leaf of paper with the date of 1740, written in 18th century handwriting, which was widely accepted by critics. This is one of the artist's most famous works, and is the culmination of his studies on the 'pastoral' theme begun many years earlier, first with the *Pastoral Scene* (in the Chicago Art Institute), and the *Idyll on the Beach* (Cologne, the Wallraf-Richartz Museum). Both of these paintings were commissioned by Marshal Schulenburg, and all three come from that joyful period of clear and bright colours that contemporaries defined as "lume solivo" (sunny light). This painting, among the most famous by Piazzetta, is universally called *The Fortune Teller*, a title suggested by the pose of the woman to the left who seems to point to the other woman's hand, but its interpretations vary widely: it can be seen politically, symbolically or even as an amorous initiation of the two youths to the right, or of one of them.
The fascination instilled by *The Fortune Teller* consists in its subtle grace, the sensual light that inundates the piece, the extremely refined chromatic harmony, the serene wisdom of the woman at the centre, who, in spite of her rustic garments is a "sister" of Tiepolo's heroines.

of the bourgeoisie, adding certain aspects from Caravaggio-influenced Rome. This painting dates to the beginning of the 1750s and is an important example of this kind of production, in which the scene is fixed with analytic precision and subtle irony.

2. Giuseppe Angeli
(Venice 1712-1798)

Il solletico

Canvas, 198 × 144 cm
Acquisition: 1995,
by purchase, (cat. 1459)
Latest restoration: 1995-96

This work came from the Berlin antiquities market, and passed on to the Pospisil collection in Venice. From there in 1990 it was moved to the Silvestro Gargantini collection in Milan, and was finally purchased by the State for the Accademia. Having studied Piazzetta, Angeli imitates similar compositions by this master, for example *The Fortune Teller*. The *Pastoral Scene* by Domenico Maggiotto (in the Kunsthalle in Hamburg), another *solletico* (tickle) scene, confirms the general diffusion of this kind of

1. Gaspare Traversi
(Naples, documented from c. 1722-Rome, 1770)

The Wounded Man

Canvas, 101 × 128 cm
Acquisition: 1956,
by purchase, (cat. 1316)

This piece is recorded in the Licata collection, and then in the collections of the Duke of Melito in Naples and of Italico Brass in Venice. Following a tradition begun in Naples by Giuseppe Bonito and in the wake of a Europe-wide trend, Traversi nurtures an increasingly clear vision of the daily life

16a

16a

4. **Vittore Ghislandi, known as 'Fra' Galgario'**
(Bergamo 1655-1743)

Portrait of Count Giovanni Battista Vailetti

Canvas, 230 × 137 cm
Acquisition: 1912, by purchase, (cat. 778)
Latest restoration: 1995

Purchased from A. Olivotti through the Export Office of Florence. This piece from 1710 was previously in the collection of the Countess Rosa Piatti Lochis, and belonged to her family for at least the latter half of the 19th century. One of the most famous portraits by the artist, it constitutes a true "still life with precious fabrics". Perhaps because of his Lombard origin, Ghislandi moved away from the frivolous and formal style of international portraiture, and instead gave Count Vailetti – portrayed in the refined intimacy of his study – an interpretation which was both idealised and realistic at the same time, with the proper rigour of an illuminist.

4

5. Giulia Lama
(Venice 1681–1747)

Judith and Holofernes

Canvas, 104 × 151 cm
Acquisition: 1976, by
purchase, (cat. 1345)

This painting came to the
Galleries from the Export
Office of Milan. Lama,
who was perhaps the
most independent of
Piazzetta's students, is
characterised by his
emphasis on forms and
his abilities with lighting,
which are the
foundational elements of
his works. For the body
of Holofernes, he based
his interpretation on a
study of a nude by
Piazzetta, in the
Accademia, which was
from before the 1740s.
This painting dates to
about the same time as
the drawing, from about
1730-1740. The biblical
heroine is captured at the
moment just prior to
when she takes action, in
an unusual position of
prayer, and is shown
along with the upturned
body of Holofernes in a
violent light to create a
composition of intense
drama and virtuosity.

5

6

6. Giuseppe Nogari
(Venice 1699–1763)

An Old Woman with a Bowl

Canvas, 52 x 41 cm
Acquisition: 1953, by
donation from Francesco
Pospisil, (cat. 1315)
Latest restoration: 1998

Alessandro Longhi's
master, Nogari specialised
in the production of
"character heads" realised
with chiaroscuro contrasts
and counter-lighting
effects, inspired by the
Nordic tradition. The *Old
Woman with a Bowl* dates
to the beginning of the
1740s and is a virtuoso
variation of the *Old
Woman with a Staff* in the
Gemäldegalerie in
Dresden, and the *Old
Woman with a Staff* in the
Prado Museum.

16a

16a

Alessandro Longhi
(Venice 1733-1813)

7. *The Family of Procurator Luigi Pisani*

Canvas, 255 × 340 cm
Acquisition: 1979, by purchase, (cat. 1355)
Latest restoration: 1996

On the globe is written "Longhj", and on the upper border of the pages of the book below to the right is the original though fragmented signature "Alessandro Abate". Again to the lower right, the inscription "Opus Pietro Longi". This work – inherited by the Bentivoglio of Aragon family and later by the Nani Mocenigo family – was carried out in 1758 together with a *pendant* (of which a fragment remains at the City Museum of Belluno, and which depicted the family of Ermolao Alvise and Andrea Pisani). On this painting are shown Doge Alvise Pisani (1664–1741) with his son Luigi the procurator, his wife Paolina Gambara and four children. surrounded by allegorical figures symbolising family virtues. The two personages in the back to the right are probably two other children of the Pisani family, while the old man dressed in black who holds a "bussolà" (a Venetian biscuit) towards the boy is probably the Abbot Giovanni Gregoretti. The allegorical figures around them allude to various family virtues; to the upper right can be seen the villa of Stra. Longhi emphasises the small slices of the father Paolo's life in Venice, adding a psychological investigation to make the painting one of the most suggestive examples of European portraiture of the time.

7

8. *Portrait of Carlo Lodoli*

Canvas, 128 × 94 cm
Acquisition: 1930, by
donation from Count A.
di Robilant, (cat. 908)
Latest restoration: 1994

The painting carries the
signature and name of
the subject at the upper
right: the Franciscan
monk Carlo Lodoli
(Venice, 1690–1761), the
famous theoretician of
the new architectural
rationalism, opposed to
the Baroque excesses and
a vehement critic of many
of his contemporary
architects. His pitiless
approach must have
garnered him quite a few
enemies, and in fact the
inscription expresses an
ironic criticism of him.
Longhi made more than
one portrait of this
controversial figure. The
chronology of this
particular work is
difficult, although it was
surely posthumous. It
should be from around
the end of the 1770s,
given its similarity with
the portrait of
Bartolomeo Ferracina in
Ca' Rezzonico, which is
from about 1770.

16a

8

Canaletto, Francesco Guardi, Giambattista Tiepolo, Pietro Longhi and Rosalba Carriera

This room was fitted between 1921 and 1923 for the display of small 18th century paintings and in 1947 Carlo Scarpa added a small narrow gallery, with a typical Venetian floor and a single velarium on the ceiling.

Canaletto, Perspective with Portico, *detail*

17

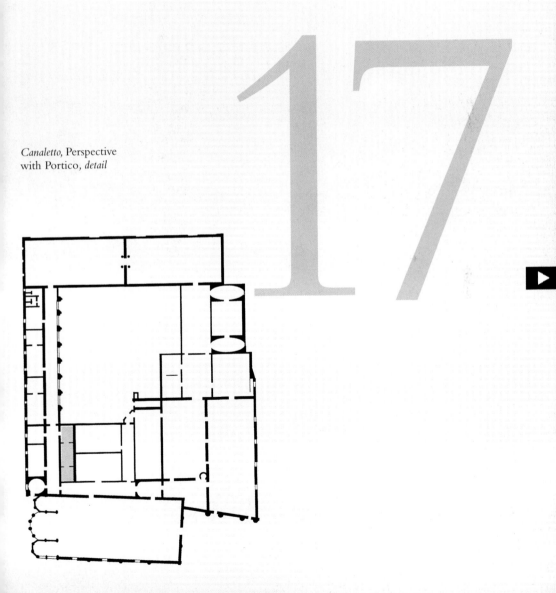

1

2

17

3

4

Giuseppe Zais
(Canale d'Agordo 1709
-Treviso 1781)

1. *Couples near a Fountain*

Canvas, 54 × 39 cm

2. *Pierrot and Couples*

Canvas, 53 × 39 cm

3. *Concert*

Canvas, 53 × 39 cm

4. *The Swing*

Canvas, 53 × 39 cm
Acquisition: 1957, from
the Palazzo Reale, (cat.
1312, 1311, 1310, 1309)
Latest restoration: 1957

The original location of
these four small paintings
is unknown. They were
inspired by French
painting of the same era,
particularly at Watteau,
which was probably
spread in Italy through
engravings and printed
illustrations. All four
works are from the artist's
mature period.

5. **Bernardo Bellotto**
(Venice 1721–Warsaw
1780)

*The Beggers' Canal and the
Scuola di San Marco*

Canvas, 41 × 59 cm
Acquisition: 1856, from
the Manfrin collection,
(cat. 494)

Latest restoration: 1990
This is probably the
painting alluded to by
Ruskin when he
described himself
painting the scene from
the same viewpoint, but
in opposition to
Canaletto. Nonetheless,
by now the work is
largely attributed to
Bellotto while in his
apprenticeship in the
studio of his uncle,
Canaletto; the work dates
to around 1740.

6. **Antonio Canal,
known as 'Canaletto',**
ascribed to (Venice 1697-
1768)

*Capriccio with Ruins and
Porta Portello in Padua*

Canvas, 61 × 76 cm
Acquisition: 1988, with
the recoveries by Rodolfo
Siviero, (cat. 1385)
Latest restoration: 1993

From the Contini-
Bonacossi collection in
Florence, the work was
removed in a clandestine
operation and then
recovered by Rodolfo
Siviero. There are twenty-
two copies of this
capriccio, which received
enormous praise. The
copies are attributed to
Canaletto's and Bellotto's
circle. The version in the
Kunsthalle in Hamburg is
probably the model upon
which they were based.
The excellent version in
Venice is from Canaletto's
work around the 1760s.

5

17

6

7

7. **Antonio Canal, known as 'Canaletto'**
(Venice 1697-1768)

Capriccio of a Colonnade

Canvas, 92 × 130 cm
Acquisition: 1807, from
the old Accademia,
(cat. 463)
Latest restoration: 1985

Trial work of acceptance
after the artist was made
professor of perspective
architecture, signed and
dated 1765. The *capriccio*
(or imaginary view), now
famous and copied many
times by Canaletto
himself, was exhibited in
1777 in Saint Mark's
Square for the *Festa della
Sensa* (The *Feast of the
Ascension*). A drawing in
the Albertini collection in
Rome is related to the
painting, and a quick
sketch in Museo Correr
could be an early idea for
the piece.

8. **Michele Marieschi**
(Venice 1710-1743)

Palazzo Courtyard with Stairs

Canvas, 36 cm × 55 cm
Acquisition: 1816,
bequest from Girolamo
Molin, (cat. 451)
Latest restoration: 1989-90

The subject was copied
in many replicas and
provides evidence of the
artist's scene painting
experience. Inspired by
the work of Marco Ricci,
but with a personal
interpretation employing
an accentuated use of the
chiaroscuro contrasts, the
work appears to be from
the end of the 1730s. The
whole "Courtyard" series
has also been attributed
to Francesco Albotto,
follower and continuator
of Marieschi.

9. **Antonio Canal, known as 'Canaletto'**
ascribed by. (Venice 1697-1768)

*Capriccio with Ruins and
Classical Buildings*

Canvas, 62 × 74 cm
Acquisition: 1988, with the
recoveries by Rodolfo
Siviero (cat. 1386)
Latest restoration: 1993

A *pendant* of painting n. 6
(cat. 1385) and of a similar
scene. The constructions
depicted in the work seem
to all be of the artist's
imagination, although they
may bring known buildings
to mind. There are sixteen
replicas of this subject; the
model on which these were
based has been recognised
as the version in the Poldi-
Pezzoli museum in Milan.
Comparison between the
one here in Venice and the
one in Milan reveals that
the Venetian version is
actually better, with more
luminous colours and a
clear descriptive analysis.

8

9

Antonio Diziani
(Venice 1737-1797)

10. *Alpine Landscape
with a Flow of Water*

Canvas, 55 × 72 cm

11. *Alpine Landscape
with a Stream and Figures*

Canvas, 55 × 72 cm
Acquisition: 1914, by
purchase, (cat. 797, 796)

Both paintings carry the
old inscription "Antonio
Diziani" on the back, and
are in fact typical examples
of the artist's landscapes.

13

14

12. Francesco Guardi
(Venice 1712-1793)

The Basin of Saint Mark's Square, with San Giorgio and the Giudecca

Canvas, 69 × 94 cm
Acquisition: 1903, donation from Prince John of Liechtenstein, (cat. 709)
Latest restoration: 1993

On the crate at the bottom on to the left is the signature: F. G. This is one of a many versions of theme treated numerous times by the artist. To the left the island of San Giorgio Maggiore, and to the right the Giudecca island with the demolished church of San Giovanni Battista of the Camaldolesi monks, and the church of the Zitelle. The painting maintains its expressive potential in spite of a certain graininess in the colour.

It is from no later than 1774, when the old onion-domed bell tower collapsed (still visible on the island of San Giorgio).

Marco Ricci
(Belluno 1676–Venice 1730)

13. *Landscape with Woodsmen and Knights*

Goat skin, 29 × 45 cm

14. *The Park of a Villa*

Goat skin, 30 × 44 cm
Acquisition: 1956, from Palazzo Reale, (cat. 1308, 1307)

These two *pendants* were painted in tempera on goat skin – a technique which creates the effect of extraordinary luminosity. They date to just before 1724, and were probably originally in the monastery of San Giorgio. The second painting, with its evocation of aspects of the daily work of a patrician villa, is a forerunner of the great *vedutisti* (view painters).

10

11

17

12

Michele Marieschi
(Venice 1710-1743)

15. *Capriccio with a Classical Arch and Goats*

Canvas, 55 × 83 cm

16. *Capriccio with a Gothic Building and an Obelisk*

Canvas, 55 × 83 cm
Acquisition: 1903, by purchase, (cat. 727, 728)

These two *pendants* are highly original and refined works. The small speckles remind the viewer of the work of Giannantonio Guardi. Other versions by the artist and his workshop exist of these two paintings, and especially of the second one.

15

16

Francesco Guardi
(Venice 1712-1793)

17. *The Anconeta Island*

Canvas, 32 × 51 cm
Acquisition: 1903, by
donation from M.
Guggenheim, (cat. 704)
Latest restoration: 1984

One of the late views by
Guardi, of which there is
a better version in the
Fogg Art Museum in
Cambridge. The painting
depicts the island of
Anconeta, also called the
'Madonnetta' because of
the small church located
on it. The piece
documents a small island
in front of San Giuliano
which does not exist
today; it was probably a
resting point for the trip
from the mainland to
Venice.

18. *Fire at S. Marcuola*

Canvas, 32 cm × 51 cm
Acquisition: 1972, by
exercise of purchase
right, (cat. 1344)
Latest restoration: 1993

This is Guardi's rendering
of a real event: the
dramatic fire at the oil
storehouse in the Ghetto,
which occurred on

November 28, 1789.
It is among the artist's
masterpieces within the
documentary style,
composed towards his
late maturity.

17

18

19. **Giambattista Tiepolo**
(Venice 1696-Madrid 1770)

Healing of a Sick Man at the Pool of Bethesda

Canvas, 62 × 45 cm
Acquisition: 1902, by purchase, (cat. 651)

An early work from around 1718-20, of excellent quality. A defect in the preparation of the canvas with oil and red ochre resulted in poor adhesion of the paint film, which is peeling away, revealing the brownish ochre behind it.

20. **Jacopo Amigoni**
(Naples? 1682?-Madrid, 1752)

Venus and Adonis

Canvas, 51 × 72 cm
Acquisition: 1910, by purchase, (cat. 743)

A special subject for Amigoni, who used it many times. This is a typical example of *boudoir* art which made Amigoni very wealthy, and is from around the 1750s.

19

20

21. **Giambattista Tiepolo?**
(Venice 1696 -Madrid 1770)

Anzia and Abrocome Meet at the Feasts of Diana

Canvas, 52 × 70 cm
Acquisition: 1911, by purchase, (cat. 740)

Originally belonged to Counts Belloni Corniani, the heirs of Francesco Algarotti. The painting was also identified as a draft for a painting by Amigoni, now lost, sent in 1744 to the court of Dresden. However, critics do not all agree with this identification, with some holding that Tiepolo could have painted Amigoni's subject for Algarotti.

21

22. **Giambattista Pittoni**
(Venice 1687–1767)

Crassus Ransacks the Temple of Jerusalem

Canvas, 54 × 72 cm
Acquisition: 1910, by
purchase, (cat. 741)

Recorded in the
Corniani Gallery of the
Algarotti family, this is
the 1743 model for the
painting commissioned
by Francesco Algarotti
for the gallery of
Augustus III in Dresden.

22

23. **Sebastiano Ricci**
(Belluno 1659–Venice 1734)

The Dream of Aesculapius

Canvas, 78 × 97 cm
Acquisition: 1929, by donation from Alessandro Contini, (cat. 910)
Latest restoration: 1993–94

A classic Rococo piece, the painting depicts Aesculapius, the god of medicine, with his trademark staff and snake. He appears on a cloud before a sleeping sick man. The work dates to the end of the 1710s.

23

17

24. **Giambattista Tiepolo**
(Venice 1696–Madrid 1770)

The Discovery of the True Cross and Saint Helena

Canvas, 51 × 49 cm
Acquisition: 1913, by purchase from Generoso Añes of Toledo, (cat. 789)
Latest restoration: 1985

This is the preparatory draft – or rather an early idea – for the large canvas by Tiepolo originally on the ceiling of the church of the Cappuccine in Castello (now in Room 11). The piece is characterised by a rapid, rotating movement that is somewhat more tranquil in the final version. Dates to around 1740.

24

25. **Francesco Fontebasso**
(Venice 1709-1769)

The Last Supper

Canvas, 70 cm × 124 cm
Acquisition: 1924, by
purchase, (cat. 880)

This piece is the *pendant*
of no. 29 (cat. 879). It is
an early work, a replica of
the painting by
Sebastiano Ricci at
Worcester College in
Oxford.

26. **Alessandro Magnasco**
(Genova c. 1667-Madrid
c. 1749)

Christ Adored by Two Nuns

Canvas, 58 × 43 cm
Acquisition: 1929, by
donation from Benno
Geiger, (cat. 909)

The small canvas is part
of the series of images
created for the worship
of the commissioners
who were particularly
sensitive to Franciscan
spirituality. Christ, risen
again and defeating Satan
– who can be seen
crushed under the clouds
– presents the
communion bowl to two
adoring nuns, perhaps
Saint Claire and another
Franciscan saint. The
piece dates to around
1721-23.

17

26

27. **Giambattista Tiepolo**
(Venice 1696–Madrid
1770)

The Glory of Saint Dominic

Canvas, 78 × 72 cm
Acquisition: 1922,
by purchase, (cat. 810)
Latest restoration: 1992-93

A draft painted for the
competition in March of
1723 for the ceiling of the
chapel of San Domenico
in the Basilica of Santi
Giovanni and Paolo. This
contest was won by
Giambattista Piazzetta.

28. **Giambattista Pittoni**
(Venice 1687–1767)

Mary Magdalene

Canvas, 45 x 36 cm
Acquisition: 1903,
by donation from W. Bode,
(cat. 707)

The painting dates to
before 1740, and was a
draft for the altar piece
originally in the church of
Santa Maria Maddalena in
Parma, today in the city's
Picture Gallery.

27

28

29

29. Francesco Fontebasso
(Venice 1709-1769)

Adoration of the Magi

Canvas, 70 × 123 cm
Acquisition: 1924, by
purchase, (cat. 879)

Like n. 15 (cat. 880) –
with which the piece
comprises a *pendant* – this
too is an early work,
strongly influenced by
Sebastiano Ricci, to whom
it was once attributed.

30. Giambattista Piazzetta
(Venice 1683-1754)

Christ on the Cross

Canvas, 70 × 48 cm
Acquisition: 1923, by
purchase from the convent
of Santa Maria della Fava,
(cat. 809)

Originally in the Filippini
Oratory connected to the
church of Santa Maria
della Fava. The painting
reveals great pictorial
elegance, although the
chiaroscuro contrasts are
accentuated by faults in
the technical execution.

30

Rosalba Carriera
(Venice 1675-1758)

31. *Portrait of a Young Nobleman*

Paper, 58 × 47 cm
Acquisition: 1816, by bequest from Girolamo Molin, (cat. 491)

With a masterful use of pastels – which were made for the artist in Rome by her friend Christian Cole – Carriera creates images almost without any preparatory drawing, giving the piece unusual luminosity thanks to her use of a dark blue paper. This portrait dates to 1727.

32. *Portrait of the French Consul, Le Blond*

Paper, 57 × 45 cm
Acquisition: 1888, bequest from Vincenzo Omoboni Astori, (cat. 490)

Father of Astori's mother, Le Blond was the General Consul of France in Venice. On September 27, 1727, Carriera wrote in her diary that she had received 16 *zecchini* for the portrait. The image of Le Blond, confidently aware of his status, is rendered incorporating the influence of Bombelli's and Cassana's portraiture, but translated into a ductile pastel technique.

31

32

33

34

33. *Portrait of a Young Woman*

Paper, 55 × 41 cm
Acquisition: 1888, bequest from Vincenzo Omoboni Astori, (cat. 496)

This work is by Carriera, and there is no indication of previous restorations, as was recently suggested. Although the woman was previously identified as the wife of Consul Le Blond, she shows none of the usual attributes of that social class, and seems rather to belong to the bourgeoisie. The portrait may be of Maria Felice Tibaldi, the daughter of the famous musician and wife of the painter Pierre Subleyras; the image is very similar to the one in a portrait painted by her husband in 1739, the year of their marriage.

34. *Portrait of Cardinal Melchiorre de Polignac*

Paper, 57 × 46 cm
Acquisition: 1888, bequest from Vincenzo Omoboni Astori, (cat. 485)

The cardinal was a friend of Astori's great-uncle; the abbot Dionisio Le Blond was his collaborator. Both visited Carriera many times in Paris, and it is possible that the portrait was begun in 1732 while Polignac was returning to Paris after being in Rome. The work was definitely completed by 14 February, 1734, when the Parisian collector Jean de Julienne wrote to Carriera in admiration of the piece.

35. *Self-portrait*

Paper, 31 × 25 cm
Acquisition: 1927, through a purchase option from the Naya Company (cat. 907)

This painting was made by the artist a few years before she fell victim to "a total loss of reason"; she would call the piece a "tragedy", meaning "that Rosalba would end tragically". Compared with the self-portrait in the English royal collection, Carriera's face appears pained and tired, almost foreshadowing the real blindness that would afflict the painter in 1746.

35

Rosalba Carriera
(Venice 1675-1758)

36. *Portrait of a Boy*

Canvas, 34 × 27 cm
Acquisition: 1888,
bequest from Vincenzo
Omoboni Astori (cat. 445)

This work, like its
pendant *Portrait of a Girl
with a Bussolà,* is undoubtedly a portrait
of the son of the French
consul Le Blond, and
reveals an image of
exquisite grace and
gentleness. It was made in
1726, just after the
portrait of the girl.

17

36

37. *Portrait of the Abbot Dionisio Le Blond*

Paper, 57 × 45 cm
Acquisition: 1888, bequest from Vincenzo Omoboni Astori, (cat. 486)
Latest restoration: in progress

Dating to 1729, as a letter from the abbot to the painter would seem to indicate, this piece reveals a greater emphasis on realism.

38. *Portrait of Girl with a Bussolà*

Paper, 34 × 27 cm
Acquisition: 1888, by bequest from Vincenzo Omoboni Astori, (cat. 444)

As Carriera wrote in her diary, the portrait was begun on May 13, 1725, while on July 22 she adds: "received a snuff-box with ten sequins (*zecchini*) from the French ambassador", which was probably payment for the work. The pastel technique renders the tender grace of the girl perfectly, depicting her with delicate analysis in the description of the refined dress, the pink ribbon in her hair, the scarf tied around her neck, and the *bussolà* – a typical Venetian biscuit – in her hand.

39. *Portrait of a Lady*

Paper, 50 × 40 cm
Acquisition: 1816, bequest from Girolamo Molin, (cat. 489)

For a long time this was mistakenly held to be a self-portrait; the identification of the woman as Anna Carlotta Gauthier, the wife of painter Jacques Aved, is also unconfirmed. The work dates to the 1730s.

37

39

38

17

175

17

40. Giambattista Tiepolo
(Venice 1696–Madrid 1770)

Transfer of the Holy House from Nazareth to Loreto

Canvas, 126 × 86 cm
Acquisition: 1930, by purchase, (cat. 911)
Latest restoration: 1993-94

A preparatory sketch for the ceiling and fresco painted by Tiepolo and Girolamo Mengozzi, known as Colonna in the church of Santa Maria di Nazareth at the Scalzi, which was destroyed in 1915 by an Austrian bomb (seven surviving fragments are on display in Room 11). This is probably the first model for the composition, for which the artist was paid 100 *zecchini* on September 13, 1743. The second model, which is more similar to the final version, is at the Getty Museum in Malibu, California. The piece celebrates the miraculous conveyance of the house of Nazareth to Loreto, where the Virgin encountered the angel Gabriel.

41

42

Pietro Longhi
(Venice 1701-1785)

41. *The Tailor*

Canvas, 60 × 49 cm
Acquisition: 1838, donation
from Girolamo Contarini,
(cat. 469)

In spite of the traditional
title, this is actually a group
portrait, as is shown by the
image of the Procurator
Nicolò Renier, elected in
1740, hanging on the wall.
Samaritana Dolfin, the wife
of Nicolò Renier's brother,
Girolamo, has just received
the tailor, with a
magnificent new dress; next
to her the daughter Maria
plays with the dog. Dating
to after *The Concert*,
between 1742–43, this piece
came to the Galleries from
the Contarini collection.

42. *The Concert*

Canvas, 60 × 49 cm
Acquisition: 1838, donation
from Girolamo Contarini,
(cat. 466)

Signed and dated Pietro
Longhi, 1741, this painting
is a masterpiece revealing
the transition from the
popular form derived from
Giuseppe Maria Crespi to
the more refined
'conversation piece' taken
from the French tradition.

43

The work confirms
Longhi's place as a "painter
of the Veneto nobility".
Some clergymen play cards
in a suggestive patrician
room, while the owners of
the house are arranged in an
unusual trio of only
violinist.

43. *The Chemist*

Canvas, 59 × 48 cm
Acquisition: 1835, donation
from Girolamo Contarini,
(cat. 467)

With the artist's signature
on the back, this is
probably his most famous
painting. The interior,
described in such intricate
detail that the *Nativity*
painting by Antonio
Balestra can be recognised,
a work now in a private
collection in Venice.
Longhi evokes an 18th
century chemist's shop
with extraordinary success.
The piece dates to around
the same time as *The
Rhinoceros* in Ca'
Rezzonico, from 1751.

17

44. *A Lady's Dressing-Room*

Canvas, 60 × 48 cm
Acquisition: 1838,
donation from Girolamo
Contarini, (cat. 464)

The focus of the
composition is the
splendid dress worn by
the lady, which shows
that the dressing ritual
was an important
moment in the day of
18th century Venetian
patrician women. From
around the same time as
the *Concert*.

45. *The Dancing Lesson*

Canvas, 60 × 48 cm
Acquisition: 1838,
donation from Girolamo
Contarini, (cat. 465)

A famous painting which
was made diffuse through
a counterpart engraving
by Flipart. The work
depicts one of the
fundamental aspects of
the education of young
Venetian patrician girls,
and dates to around the
1740s or 50s.

44

46. *The Fortune-Teller*

Canvas, 60 × 48 cm
Acquisition: 1838,
donation from Girolamo
Contarini, (cat. 468)

The inscription, top right
"Per Piovan/in San
Fantin/pre' Zuanne",
probably refers to the
parochial election in San
Fantin of don Giovanni
(Zuanne) Pecchion,
which occurred on
August 6, 1759, the *post
quem* date for the
completion of this piece.

46

Trials Works by the Academicians

This hallway was constructed in the early 19th century and redesigned by Carlo Scarpa in 1953. He closed off two windows and added a single door onto the balcony. The wooden footing was eliminated, the ceiling was lowered and new skylights were opened. The display cases with the Canova sketches were added in 1949. Originally the room was to be used for displaying drawings in rotation, but later trial works from the old Accademia at the Fonteghetto della Farina were brought here.

Antonio Maria Visentini,
Architectural Invention,
detail

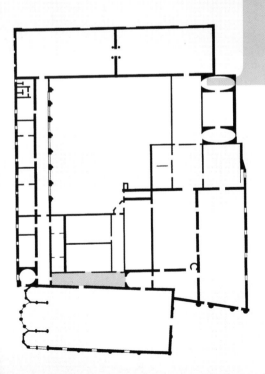

1. Giuseppe Zais
(Canale d'Agordo 1709 -Treviso 1781)

Landscape with a Fountain

Canvas, 132 × 80 cm
Acquisition: 1807, from the old Accademia, (cat. 447)
Latest restoration: 1962

On the left, at the bottom, are the artist's initials. With this painting he applied, in 1765, to be accepted into the Accademia, but was not admitted until September 11, 1774.

2. Francesco Battaglioli
(Modena, c. 1720-Venice, records until 1797)

Architectural Perspective

Canvas, 131 × 56 cm
Acquisition: 1807, from the old Accademia, (cat. 461)
Latest restoration: 1987

Chosen in 1777 with other canvases from the old Accademia to be exhibited at the *Fiera della Sensa* fair in Saint Mark's Square. The painting was completed by Battaglioli

to mark his nomination to the Accademia in 1776. The inventive work reveals his talents for perspective and his familiarity with Canaletto's work.

3. Giuseppe Moretti
(originally from Val Camonica, active in Venice during the second half of the 18th century)

Perspective Study

Canvas, 130 × 56 cm
Acquisition: 1807, from the old Accademia, (cat. 471)
Latest restoration: 1987

Displayed at the *Fiera della Sensa* in 1777, this painting was submitted by Moretti for his entrance into the Accademia in 1776. Canaletto's influence is evident, especially in the figures that recall those in the *Campo San Giacomo at Rialto* in the State Museum of Berlin.

4. Pietro Gaspari
(Venezia 1720-1785)

Architectural Perspective

Canvas, 131 × 79 cm
Acquisition: 1807, from the old Accademia, (cat. 470)
Latest restoration: 1987

To the lower left on the base is the signature and the date of 1775. This is the "pièce de reception" for Gaspari's acceptance into the Accademia, and is a good representation of virtuosity of the "perspective" trend in the 1700s.

5. Antonio Joli
(Modena, c. 1700-Naples, 1777)

Perspective with Ancient Baths

Canvas, 130 × 93 cm
Acquisition: 1807, from the old Accademia, (cat. 450)
Latest restoration: 1987

"Pièce de reception" for Joli's acceptance into the Accademia, to which he was elected on February 13, 1756, this is a typical example of the artist's painting. After working as a scene painter in

2

3

Modena until about 1740, he went to Venice to become one of the major exponents of "perspective" painting, working also in Germany, London and Madrid.

6. Antonio Maria Visentini
(Venice 1688-1782)

Architectural Invention

Canvas, 135 × 94 cm
Acquisition: 1807, from the old Accademia, (cat. 448)

The signature is written at the left on the edge of the balustrade. A group of architects intent on measuring the ruins of an ancient building stand in a portico that recalls Veronese and Palladio. Their very presence, along with the drawing tools, the plumb line, Palladio's *Trattato* at easy reach, all allude to the teaching of architectural perspective as an essential element of painting. The work was connected with the institution of the Perspective Chair at the Accademia, to which Visentini was appointed in 1764, but which was only confirmed in 1772. The work was probably completed after this date, and is recorded in 1777, when it was displayed at the *Fiera della Sensa*.

4

5

18

6

7. Domenico Fedeli, known as 'Maggiotto'
(Venice 1713-1794)

Allegory of the Academy

Canvas, 130 × 92 cm
Acquisition: 1807, from the old Accademia, (cat. 443)
Latest restoration: 1960

The signature is to the lower right. This painting was probably donated to the Accademia in 1763. The artist was admitted to the Accademia in 1756; this work is significant for its refined academic nature, in which Maggiotto effectively translates the teachings of Piazzetta.

8. Michelangelo Morlaiter
(Venezia 1729-1806)

Venice Awards the Fine Arts

Canvas, 131 × 183 cm
Acquisition: 1807, from the old Accademia, (cat. 425)
Latest restoration: 1960

Displayed at the *Fiera della Sensa* in 1777, the work had most likely been donated to the Accademia in 1756 by Morlaiter when he was admitted. The figure of Venice is depicted awarding prize-medals to Painting, Sculpture and Architecture. The 'academic' subject echoes a neo-classical aspect.

9. Francesco Maggiotto
(Venice 1750-1805)

Allegory of Painting

Canvas, 130 × 115 cm
Acquisition: 1807, from the old Accademia, (cat. 442)

The signature is to the right on the sheet under the palette. The work was the obligatory donation made by the artist in 1769 for his election into the Accademia in 1768. While the seated woman symbolises Painting, the standing woman is an allegory for Nature. The boy to the right represents Drawing. The influence of new neo-classical theories is evident in the work.

10. Pietro Longhi
(Venice 1702-1785)

The Philosopher Pythagoras

Canvas, 130 × 91 cm
Acquisition: 1807, from the old Accademia, (cat. 479)

The signature is written at the lower left. The title is the one used by Pietro's son Alessandro for the engraving made of this painting. The work was completed as an entrance piece for the Accademia, which selected Longhi in its first group of students in February of 1756. Between the end of 1762 and the first months of 1763, it appears that – following their recall in May of 1761

– on November 14 of 1762 it was decided to send the canvases back to Longhi and to the other painters who had not yet completed the work required by the statute, with the injunction that the works were to be completed within six months. Longhi's position as an instructor on painting nudes evidently influenced his choice of subject.

11. Francesco Zuccarelli
(Pitigliano, 1702-Florence, 1788/89)

Landscape with John the Baptist

Canvas, 132 × 94 cm
Acquisition: 1807, from the old Accademia, (cat. 458)
Latest restoration: 1960

Zuccarelli was elected into

7

9

8

10

11

the Accademia on January 16 of 1763, and at the same time was also chosen to be an instructor. The painting was originally in the old Accademia, and must have been completed immediately after his appointment. Although the figure of John the Baptist appears conventional, the landscape reveals intense pictorial accents.

12. **Pierantonio Novelli**
(Venice 1729-1804)

Drawing, Colour and Invention

Canvas, 130 × 132 cm
Acquisition: 1807, from the old Accademia, (cat. 762)
Latest restoration: 1993

At the bottom-right is the inscription with the signature and date of 1776. Admitted into the Accademia in 1768, Novelli submitted this neo-classical inspired work in 1771 and revised it again in 1776.

13. **Alessandro Longhi**
(Venice 1733-1813)

Painting and Merit

Canvas, 128 × 93 cm
Acquisition: 1807, from the old Accademia, (cat. 493)
Latest restoration: 1958

The signature is painted on the spine of the book. This allegorical painting refers to the artist's acceptance into the Accademia in 1759 but dates to the end of the 1770s.
The artist made an engraving of the painting and dedicated it to John Udny, the English Consul in Venice in 1761 and from 1773-75.

18

12

13

Antonio Canova
(Possagno 1757-Venice 1822)

14. Fighters

Terracotta, 30 × 31 cm
Acquisition: 1807, from the old Accademia, (cat. 549)
Latest restoration: 1979

The signature is painted on the base. With this group from 1775, Canova won second prize at the first sculpture competition held by the Accademia. The subject is taken from the old plaster copy in the Filippo Farsetti collection (which was generously made available to the students); the original is in the Uffizi in Florence. The small terracotta was made when Canova was only 18 years old, and established him as the last great exponent of 18th century Venetian figurative culture.

14

18

15. *Apollo*

Terracotta, height 61 cm
Acquisition: 1807, from the
old Accademia, (cat. 550)
Latest restoration: 1987

The signature is painted
on the base. Antonio
Canova submitted this
sculpture on March 30,
1779 to apply for
membership of the
Accademia; he was
unanimously accepted on
April 5, 1779. With this
sculpture, Canova
demonstrates that in spite
of his 18th century
education, he was also
quite familiar with the
work of Bernini. Many of
Bernini's models were in
the Farsetti collection,
which Canova frequented
assiduously.

16. *Pietà*

Clay, 21 × 34 cm
Acquisition: 1911,
by purchase, (cat. 552)
Latest restoration: 1980

The signature is engraved
on the base at the centre.
After Canova died, this
work was passed down to
his student Baruzzi who
donated it in 1831 to the
clergyman Gardenghi.
Gardenghi's brother gave
it to Cardinal Baruffi, the
Bishop of Imola, who
then left it to his heirs.
A late work based on a
common subject, it
nonetheless maintains the
quick spirit of invention
found in the artist's
earlier works.

18

15

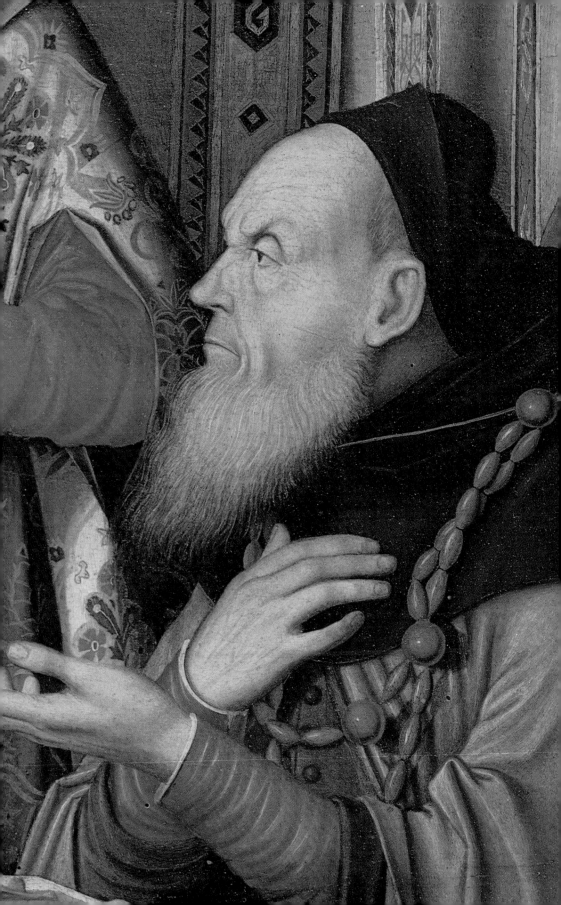

Bartolomeo Montagna, Giovanni Agostino da Lodi and Boccaccio Boccaccino

This is a corridor which connects with rooms 20 and 21, showing 15th century "story" cycles. The platform at the back with the sash window, from which one can admire the view of the Palladio convent, was designed by Carlo Scarpa in 1947.

Marco Marziale, Supper in Emmaus, *detail*

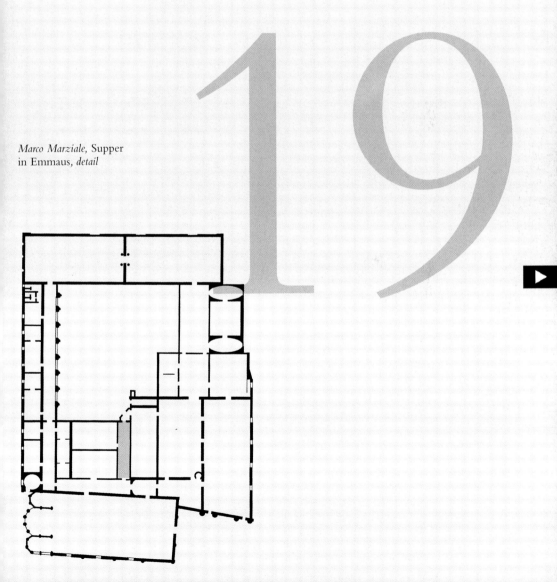

1. **Giovanni Agostino da Lodi**
(Active from the end of the 15th century, with records from until c. 1520)
Washing of the Feet

Panel, 132 × 111 cm
Acquisition: 1856, purchase from the Manfrin collection, (cat. 599)
Latest restoration: 1991-92

The date of 1500 is painted on Saint Peter's stool. The work is inspired by the arrangement of the heads and the physical characterisations of the *Last Supper* by Leonardo da Vinci, and there are also numerous references to Bramantino. The original location of the work is unknown, but it was probably made for Venice since it is well known and was often imitated there.

1

2

3

4

2. **Pietro de Saliba**?
(active at the end of the 15th and the beginning of the 16th centuries)

Christ at the Column

Panel, 40 × 33 cm
Acquisition: 1856, by purchase from the Manfrin collection, (cat. 589)
Latest restoration: 1993

This painting was part of a group of works depicting the bust of Christ crowned with thorns and against a column with a rope around his neck; the works were all based on a model by Antonello which may be his *Christ,* now at the Louvre.

3. **Antonello de Saliba**
(Messina c. 1467-c. 1535)

Annunciation

Panel, 47 × 34 cm
Acquisition: 1812, following the Napoleonic suppressions, (cat. 590)
Latest restoration: 1993

Originally in the Sala dell'Ante-Collegio at the Doge's Palace, the work was part of a group of paintings donated to the Republic by Bertucci Contarini. Although it was long believed to be the work of Antonella da Messina, it is instead a copy of the *Annunciation* by the master in the Galleria Nazionale in Palermo, completed around 1476-1477. The presence of Venetian motifs derived from Bellini and Montagna confirmed that the piece was by Antonello de Saliba (the son of a brother-in-law of Antonello da Messina), who resided in Venice from 1480-1497.

4. **Marco Basaiti**?
(Venice, 1470/75-1530)

Saint Jerome

Panel, 54 × 42 cm
Acquisition: 1816, bequest from Girolamo Molin, (cat. 107)
Latest restoration: 1993

A work for private devotion, the subject was copied many times by Basaiti; this may be from the artist's later period.

5. **Marco Basaiti**, attr.
(Venice, 1470/75-post 1530)

Christ between Two Angels

Panel, 39 × 103 cm
Acquisition: 1812-14, following the Napoleonic suppressions, (cat. 108)
Latest restoration: 1993

This piece came to the Accademia galleries together with *Saint James the Apostle* and *Saint Anthony the Abbot* from the convent of Santa Maria dei Miracoli. It is traditionally attributed to Basaiti, and the most recent restoration revealed its extraordinarily high quality. The representation of Christ's dead body – typical of Venetian painters – is deeply rooted in Byzantine iconography. Similarities are also in evidence between this work and Carpaccio's *Mourning of the Dead Christ* in the Berlin State Museum.

19

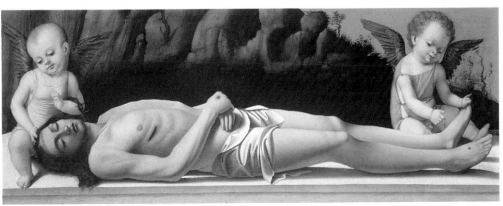

5

6

7

8

6. Bartolomeo Cincani, known as 'Montagna'
(Vicenza c. 1449-1523)

Saint Peter

Panel, 60 × 39 cm
Acquisition: 1971, by purchase, (cat. 1343)
Latest restoration: 1979

On the scroll held in the mouth of the dog is written "esto fidelis" (be faithful). Because of its affinity with the frescos in the Verona church of Santi Nazaro e Celso, the work has been attributed to Mantegna since 1871, when it was recorded in the Papafava collection in Padua. The painting dates to around 1505. The

work reveals the artist's extraordinary ability to bring together the human figure, architecture and landscape. The influence of Antonello da Messina is enriched with aspects inspired by Giovanni Bellini, especially evident in the enchanting background of the Veneto mainland: among the various buildings one can recognise the façade of the Duomo of Vicenza and the Arena of Pola.

Jacopo Parisati, known as 'da Montagnana'
(records from 1458-Padua, 1499)

7. *Herald Angel*

Panel, 185 × 74 cm

8. *Annunciation*

Panel, 185 cm × 76 cm
Acquisition: 1812, following the Napoleonic suppressions, (cat. 606, 608)
Latest restoration: 1984

Originally in the church of Monte Artone (Padua), these paintings must once have formed a single painting. A central part measuring about 110 cm appears to have been cut out, evident also from the interruption of the

bed with the red canopy. Vasari (1550) also notes that "il Montagnana [...] fece in Padova a Santa Maria di Monte Artone una tavola nella chiesa" ("Montagnana [...] painted a panel in the church of Santa Maria di Monte Artone in Padua"). The work, which was completed between 1494 and 1497, represents the artist's translation of the teachings of Mantegna into a more refined decorativism.

9. Boccaccio Boccaccino
(Ferrara? before August 22, 1466-Cremona, c. 1524/25)

Marriage of Saint Catherine, with Saints Rose, Peter and John the Baptist, The Announcement to the Shepherds, The Flight into Egypt and The Magi on Horseback

Panel, 87 × 143 cm
Acquisition: 1838, donation from Girolamo Contarini, (cat. 600)
Latest restoration: 1993

The signature is at the lower right. The work was completed at the end of the artist's stay in Venice (1506), with many elements taken from Bellini, Carpaccio and Giorgione, and even some echoes of the *Madonna of the Rosary* by Dürer, displayed in 1506 in the church of San Bartolomeo.

19

9

12

10

11

Marco Basaiti
(Venice, 1470/75–post 1530)

10. *Saint James the Apostle*

Panel, 114 × 35 cm

11. *Saint Anthony the Abbot*

Panel, 114 × 35 cm
Acquisition: 1812-14,
following the Napoleonic
suppressions, (cat. 68/A, 68)
Latest restoration: 1993

The two panels signed
"Marcus and Basait. p."
("Basaiti painted") on their
respective pedestals appear
to be of different quality, but
still similar in style to Marco
di Oggiono, who was called
to make some paintings for
the Milanesi confraternity at
the Frari in 1497 and 1498,
for whom Basaiti was also
completing the large altarpiece of Saint Ambrose after
the death of Alvise Vivarini.

12. Marco Marziale
(records from 1493 to 1507)

Supper in Emmaus

Panel, 122 × 141 cm
Acquisition: 1838, donation
from Girolamo Contarini,
(cat. 76)
Latest restoration: 1993

The signature and date (1506)
are on a scroll on the leg of
the table. The iconographic
source of the subject, with its
Dürer-inspired details, must
have been the lost *Supper in
Emmaus* by Giovanni Bellini
mentioned by Vasari (1568) in
the Giorgio Cornaro
collection, known now from
the engraving made of it by

Pietro Monaco and the copy
(made with collaborators) in
the Church of San Salvador.
Another variation was
painted by Marziale in 1507,
now in the State Museum in
Berlin.

13. Anonymous Veneto painter from the beginning of the 16th century

*Apparition of the Crucifixes
of Mount Ararat in the Church
of Sant'Antonio in Castello*

Canvas, 121 cm × 174 cm
Acquisition: 1838, from the
warehouse of *Commenda*
following the Napoleonic
suppressions, (cat. 91)

Originally in the Church of
Sant'Antonio in Castello, the
work depicts the vision seen
by Francesco Ottoboni, the

prior of the convent, when he
invoked the aid of the Martyrs
of Mount Ararat (Room 2,
cat. 89) during a plague in
1511. The Martyrs appeared to
him in a dream entering in a
procession into the church
lead by Saint Peter. The
interior, with the wooden
'barco', or nuns' gallery, the ex
voto, the altar and the
polyptychs offers us an
interesting image of a Venetian
church at the beginning of the
1500s – still Gothic in style,
but undergoing remodelling.
It was originally attributed to
Carpaccio (Boschini, 1664),
but this attribution has recently
been called into question. In
effect, the general repainting
on the work – which does
however essentially keep to the
drawing underneath – makes
any critical evaluation difficult.

19

13

"Miracles of the Relic of the Cross"

This room was already constructed in 1940. Seven years later the canvases with the "Miracles of the Cross" were placed here provisionally; in 1959-1960 Carlo Scarpa completed the arrangement, which has remained practically unchanged ever since. The cycle originally served to adorn the walls of the Sala dell'Albergo also known as Room of the Cross in the Scuola di San Giovanni Evangelista, where there is still a relic of the Holy Cross on display, donated to the guild in 1369 by Filippo de Mezióres, the Great Chancellor of the Kingdom of Cyprus. There were originally ten canvases, including *The Miracle of the Vendramin Ships* by Pietro Perugino, completed in 1494. Unfortunately only eight are on display at the Accademia; Perugino's canvas – composed while he was in Venice working in the Doge's Palace – was destroyed and replaced in 1588. The most detailed record on these canvases is a pamphlet from 1590 which describes the "Miracles", supplying the artist's name and year of completion of the paintings. The Scuola di San Giovanni Evangelista was suppressed by Napoleonic decree in 1806, and the paintings were delivered to the Accademia in 1820, where they were displayed separately at various times until they were finally brought together in 1947.

Vittore Carpaccio, Miracle of the Relic of the Cross at the Rialto Bridge, *detail*

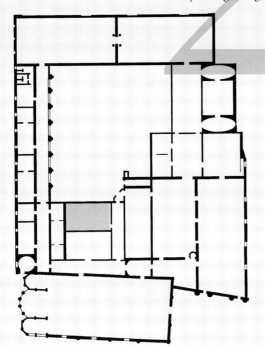

1. **Vittore Carpaccio**
(Venice? c. 1460–1525/26)

Miracle of the Relic of the true Cross at the Rialto Bridge or *The Heading of the Possessed Man*

Canvas, 371 × 392 cm
Acquisition: 1820, following the Napoleonic suppressions, (cat. 566)
Latest restoration: 1990–91

This canvas was completed in 1494 for the east wall of the Albergo to the right of the altar, and narrates the miraculous healing of a possessed man. The work was obtained by Francesco Querini – the patriarch of Grado – through the reliquary of the sacred cross. In 1544, after hearing the opinion of "prudente messer Tizian pictor" ("the sagacious painter Titian"), a part was cut at the bottom left near the opening of the door which led to the "Albergo Nuovo", built during this period. The gap was then arbitrarily integrated. The artist synthesises three fundamental moments: the procession on the bridge, the entrance of the patriarch, and the miracle which takes place on the loggia. But even this event is overshadowed by the representation of the city itself. The bridge is still the wooden one constructed in 1458, with the drawbridge part at the centre to allow larger boats to pass. This collapsed in 1524, and was replaced by the present one made of stone. On the left can be seen the emblem of the Storione Albergo and the loggia, where the market's patrons would gather. On the right, the Fondaco dei Tedeschi, which was destroyed by fire in 1505, Ca' da Mosto with its portico which still exists today, the campanile of San Giovanni Cristostomo and the one of Santi Apostoli, rebuilt in 1672. The contrast with the analytic realism of the other canvases further reveals Carpaccio's descriptive abilities and his emphasis on chromatics.

2. **Giovanni Mansueti**
(records from 1485–1526/27)

The Miraculous Healing of the Daughter of Benvegnudo

Canvas, 361 × 299 cm
Acquisition: 1820, following the Napoleonic suppressions, (cat. 562)
Latest restoration: 1990

This work illustrates the miraculous event that took place in 1414, when the daughter of Benvegnudo, who had been immobile since birth, was miraculously healed when touched by three candles that her father had placed near the relic. Completed after 1502, this canvas has great historical interest, and recalls techniques employed by Carpaccio on his *Saint Ursula Cycle* (Room 21), but also imitated by other artists, such as Paolo Veronese, who will mimic the 'dead stairs' and the arcades framing the narration in his *Christ in the House of Levi* (Room 10, cat. 203).

3. **Gentile Bellini**
(Venice 1429–1507)

Miracle of the Relic of the Cross on San Lorenzo Bridge

1

Canvas, 326 × 435 cm
Acquisition: 1820,
following the Napoleonic
suppressions, (cat. 568)
Latest restoration: 1989–90

At the centre are the
signature and date (1500).
According to legend,
between 1370 and 1382,
during a procession to
the church of San
Lorenzo, the relic
accidentally fell into the
canal, and only the Great
Guardian Andrea
Vendramin could grab it.
The painting is also
interesting for its
depiction of the urban
scene. To the left Caterina
Cornaro and her ladies
witness the scene, while
the five people kneeling
to the right have been
identified as members of
the painter's family, but it
is more likely that they
are high ranking
members of the Scuola.

2

3

Gentile Bellini
(Venice 1429-1507)

4. *Miraculous Healing of Pietro de' Ludovici*

Canvas, 368 × 263 cm
Acquisition: 1820,
following the Napoleonic
suppressions, (cat. 563)
Latest restoration: 1992

The signature – not the original – is on an inscription on the steps, repeating an ancient tradition. It is unclear if the graft on the lower part of the work – rather rough and repainted – was in relation to the placement of a doorway. The work depicts how Pietro de' Ludovici was healed of his quartan fever after touching a candle that had been near the relic of the saint he was worshipping. The painting was probably completed in 1501 using drawings by Gentile's father Jacopo, and with extensive graphic work by Gentile himself.

5. *Procession in Saint Mark's Square*

Canvas, 373 × 745 cm
Acquisition: 1820,
following the Napoleonic
suppressions, (cat. 567)
Latest restoration: 1988-89

At the bottom in the centre of the painting can be read the date 1496 and the artist's signature. Two large grafts at the ends of the lower part probably correspond to two doorways on the front wall of the altar (Ridolfi 1648); they were filled when the painting was moved to opposite the windows after the 17th century remodelling project by Massari. The first of Gentili's paintings for the cycle, it depicts the procession taking place in Saint Mark's Square on the Feast of Saint Mark. All the schools participated in this event with their respective relics. In particular, the painting describes the event that took place on April 25, 1444, when the Brescian merchant Jacopo de' Salis prayed for and received help for his gravely wounded son. But this miracle is described with less attention than the square itself, however, which is shown here as it appeared before the changes made to it in the 16th century. The Basilica still glisters with its original mosaics, of which only one exists today. The arches and the Porta della Carta (the main door) radiate with gold and various colours. To the right, next to the ancient campanile appears the Orseolo Hospice, demolished about 50 years later when Sansovino redesigned the Square, here still with its pink brick paving and built the Procuratie Nuove.

4

20

5

6

6. **Benedetto Rusconi, known as 'Diana'**
(Venice c. 1460-1525)

Miracle of the Holy Cross

Canvas, 371 × 150 cm
Acquisition: 1820,
following the Napoleonic
suppressions, (cat. 565)
Latest restoration: 1990

This painting depicts an
episode that took place
on March 10, 1480, when
the son of Ser Alvise
Finetti was healed after
falling from a loft. The
work reveals the influence
of the most advanced
artists of the time,
especially Giorgione and
Lotto, and was probably
completed by 1510.

7. **Lazzaro Bastiani**
(Venice c. 1425/30-1512)

*Offering of the Relic of the
Cross to the Members of the
Scuola di San Giovanni
Evangelista*

Canvas, 324 × 441 cm
Acquisition: 1820,
following the Napoleonic
suppressions, (cat. 561)
Latest restoration: 1992

The painting shows
Filippo de Mezières
offering the miraculous
relic. The episode is
depicted from the
exterior, and provides a
valuable testimony of
buildings which were
later modified or
destroyed. We can
recognise the old façade
of the church of San
Giovanni Evangelista
with its portico which
was later demolished. To
the left on the side of the

Scuola can be seen the
circular windows – the
existence of which recent
restoration projects have
also confirmed – and the
raising of the large hall by
about 2 metres, which
occurred in 1495. In this
same year, according to
the 1590 pamphlet (see
the introduction to the
room), Bastiani painted
this work, probably
immediately after the
alterations.

8. **Giovanni Mansueti**
(records from 1485-1526/27)

*Miracle of the Relic of the
Cross in Campo San Lio*

Canvas, 322 × 463 cm
Acquisition: 1820,
following the Napoleonic
suppressions, (cat. 564)
Latest restoration: 1990

On the inscription held by
the person on the left
bringing a hand towards his
hat – probably a self-portrait
– can be read the signature
of the painter, who
considered himself a disciple
of Bellini. The extraordinary
event occurred in 1474
during the funeral of a
member of the confraternity
who had not had enough
faith in the relic; the cross
became incredibly heavy
and had to be entrusted to
the parish priest of San Lio.
Probably painted in 1494,
Mansueti must have used a
preparatory drawing by
Gentile Bellini, now in the
Uffizi. The writing on the
scroll at the far right of the
side of the church is curious:
"Casa da fitar ducati 5"
("House for rent, 5 ducats").

20

7

8

Vittore Carpaccio's "Legend of Saint Ursula"

In this room, which once held the collection of Girolamo Contarini, the *Saint Ursula* cycle by Carpaccio was installed between 1921 and 1923. From 1959-60 Carlo Scarpa remodelled the room, lowering the paintings, which he supported and surrounded by a strip of light oak with a thin gilt border.

The altar-piece, set slightly back and illuminated from the side by a new source of light, was separated from the canvases by wooden screens. The works come from the Scuola di Sant'Orsola – today the canonry of the church of Santi Giovanni e Paolo, which had decided in 1488 to decorate its seat with "the stories of the Madonna Saint Ursula". Carpaccio composed nine paintings dating from 1490 to 1495. The stylistic differences of the canvases – which have also undergone numerous restorations and changes – are attributed to the many assistants. In fact, the artist made wide use of preparatory cartoons which were placed on the canvas using the dusting system – a task partly shared by various assistants. Based on an affirmation in *De origine, situ urbis Venetae* by Marin Sanudo, who noted in 1493 that "... among the interesting things of this city is the chapel of Saint Ursula at San Zuanne Pollo [Santi Giovanni e Paolo], and the beautiful figures and stories in it", it is likely that most of the cycle had been completed by that time. The cycle narrates the story of Ursula, taken rather liberally from the *Legenda Aurea*, written by Jacopo da Varagine in 1475. Ursula, the Christian Breton princess, agrees to marry the prince Hereus of England, provided that he is baptised. Together they go on a pilgrimage to Rome and many young women accompany them. They arrive in Cologne with the Pope himself and are slain by the Huns – an event that had been foretold to Ursula in a dream.

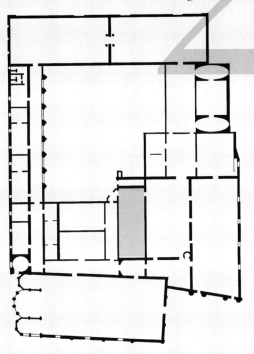

Vittore Carpaccio, The Arrival of the English Ambassadors (at the court of the King of Brittany), *detail*

Vittore Carpaccio
(Venice? c. 1460-1525/26)

1. *The Arrival of the English Ambassadors*

Canvas, 278 cm × 589 cm
Acquisition: 1812, following the Napoleonic suppressions, (cat. 572)
Latest restoration: 1983

At the lower centre is the inscription: "op. victoris/carpatio/veneti". The works do not observe the logical sequence of the story, which actually begins with this canvas. The piece condenses three scenes, set off by three architectural elements: the arrival of the ambassadors at the court of Brittany and the presentation of the Prince Hereus's marriage proposal; Ursula in her room relates to her father the marriage conditions she requires while the nurse waits at the foot of the stairs. As on the canvas with the *Meeting and the Departure of the Betrothed* (n. 4), at the centre is a person with the emblem on his sleeve of the Compagnia della Calza degli Ortolani, a guild of pleasure-seeking nobles. A part of the lower area of the painting was cut for a door, possibly in 1647. On this occasion, the face of a pageboy was probably covered, to the right, which the tampering severed from its body and which the latest restoration brought to light. The building in the centre is inspired by the Temple of Jerusalem, from xylographies by Reeuwich, while the influence of Perugino, who was in Venice in 1494, is evident in the arches to the left. Preparatory drawings are kept at Christ Church Library in Oxford, the Museo Nazionale in La Valletta and at the British Museum.

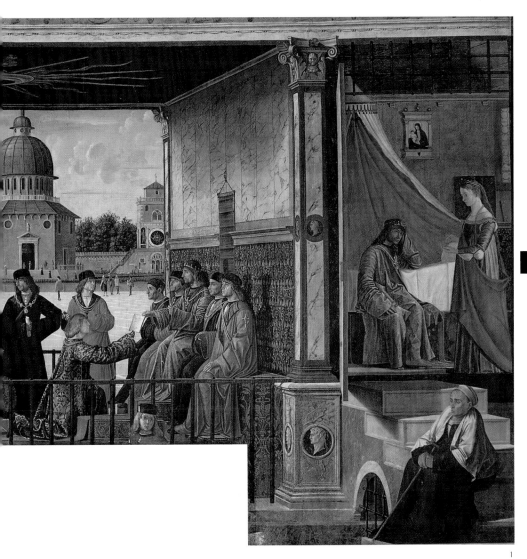

2. Dismissal of the Ambassadors

Canvas, 281 × 252 cm
Acquisition: 1812,
following the Napoleonic
suppressions, (cat. 573)
Latest restoration: 1984

At the lower left is the
inscription: "victoris car/
veneti/opus". The
extraordinary Lombard
styled interior is an
excellent example of
perspective science and
chromatic awareness.
Ursula's father concludes
the diplomatic
negotiations, consigning
the reply for the King of
England to the
ambassadors. This letter
was very likely to have
been written by the scribe
in the background, whose
role is, therefore, that of
an "artistic chronicler"
(Sgarbi) of history. The
painting is perhaps the
most complex of the
cycle, and is especially
interesting for the
elegance of the decorative
motifs and the emphasis
placed on the spatial and
architectural aspects.

21

2

3. *The Return of the Ambassadors*

Canvas, 297 × 526 cm
Acquisition: 1812, following the Napoleonic suppressions, (cat. 574)
Latest restoration: 1983

At the lower left is the inscription: "victoris/ ca ... tio/ veneti/opus", and on the base of the pennant is an indication of a restoration in 1623. The last of the negotiations: the return home of the English messengers with Ursula's reply is announced near a pier by a small page-boy and by a 'steward', whose job it was to introduce the ambassadors to the Doge's banquet to the accompaniment of musicians. The ceremony is thus taken from the one in use in the Venetian Republic. Here, history and news overlap, evidenced by the young English messenger advancing to the left with the insignia of the Venetian *Compagnia della Calza* society. The youth behind him seems to occupy the ideal centre of the composition, where the images of the city are scenically rendered. The towers to the left seem to be those of the Arsenale.

3

21

207

4. *Meeting and Departure of the Betrothed*

Canvas, 279 × 610 cm
Acquisition: 1812, following the Napoleonic suppressions, (cat. 575)
Latest restoration: 1983-84

At the base of the pennant on an inscription are the signature and date of 1495: "victoris carpatioi/veneti-opus/MCCCCLXXXXV. This canvas is divided into three episodes: the prince takes leave of his parents before departing; the betrothed couple bid farewell to the king and queen, and finally they set sail on the ships which will bring them to Rome. In the background are shown the locations of the story: on the left is medieval England, while on the right is Renaissance Brittany, with the tower of the Knights of Rhodes and the tower of Saint Mark in Crete, taken from woodcuts by Reeuwich (1486). These buildings would seem to confirm the hypothesis that the story of Ursula alludes to that of Caterina Cornaro, the queen of Cyprus. The two youths at the centre are members of the *Compagnia della Calza*. The seated one has the emblem of the Ortolani or the Zardinieri on his sleeve, and the initials F.Z.: (Fratres Zardinieri). and on a legging the initials S.A. (societas Amicorum). The standing one holds a scroll on which can be read the letters: "n. l. d. d. v. v. g. v. i.", which stand for "nicolaus lauretanus donum dedit ursulae virginis gloriosa virginibusque inclitis". It is thus likely that the commissioner – at least of this work – was Nicola Loredan.

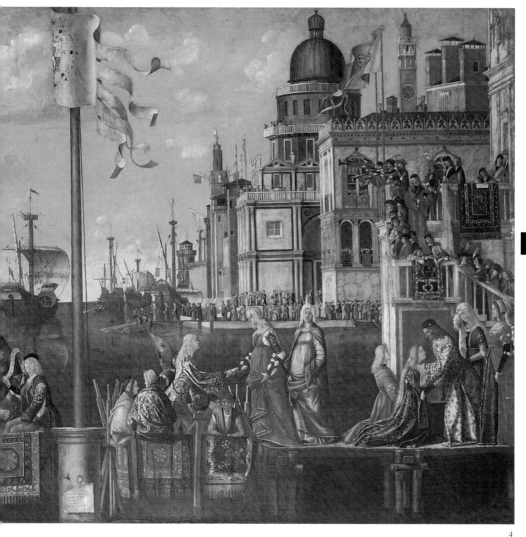

4

209

5. *The Dream of Ursula*

Canvas, 273 × 267 cm
Acquisition: 1812, following the Napoleonic suppressions, (cat. 578)
Latest restoration: 1984

On the inscription at the foot of the bed is the apocryphal inscription, but which surely respects the original version: "victor carp/f/ MCCCCLXXXXV". This is the most damaged canvas, so much so that it was only exhibited in 1852 in order to ensure the unity of the cycle. Here Ursula receives the announcement of martyrdom from an angel while she sleeps in her room. This work reveals a strong Flemish influence, with one of the most suggestive interiors of Renaissance painting. The light shed by the dawn shows all the objects in the room, laden with symbolic significance, such as the myrtle and clove plants on the biforate window which allude to conjugal love and faithfulness. On the base of the statue of Hercules above the door is the inscription "diva f. av. /st. a" (divine announcements are propitious), indicating that the prophesy is actually favourable, in spite of its apparent dramatic nature.
A beautiful preparatory drawing is at the Uffizi in Florence, and shows an additional two biforate windows in the back wall.

21

5

6. *The Pilgrims Meet the Pope Under the Walls of Rome*

Canvas, 279 × 305 cm
Acquisition: 1812, following the Napoleonic suppressions, (cat. 577)
Latest restoration: 1984

On the scroll is the inscription: "victoris/carpatio-veneti/opus". After a long voyage, the pilgrims have reached the gates of Rome where they meet the Pope before the Castle of Sant'Angelo, in accordance with an old diplomatic tradition "for important visitors arriving on the via Aurelia" (Zorzi). The pontefice decides to join the royal entourage after the baptism of Hereus and the coronation of the couple. The ceremony replicates a Doge's procession, as indicated by the umbrella – a typical attribute of the highest city authorities of Venice. Carpaccio was probably influenced by a Giovanni Bellini painting from the lost cycle with the stories of Alexander III in the Doge's Palace. The figure in the red toga to the right of the pope – a *didascalos*, someone who would point out the more salient elements in plays – has been identified as the Venetian humanist Ermolao Barbaro, who died in the Republic's disfavour in 1493; this fact makes it unlikely that the artist would portray him before that date.

21

6

7

7. Arrival in Cologne

Canvas, 279 × 254 cm
Acquisition: 1812,
following the Napoleonic
suppressions, (cat. 579)
Latest restoration: 1984

To the lower left on a
scroll is the inscription:
"op. victoris/carpatio/
veneti-MCCCCLXXXX.
m/septembris" (1490, in
September). This is surely
the first painting made by
the artist, evident not only
because of the date, but
also because of the
apparent difficulty in
articulating the
simultaneous
representation of many
subjects in the available
space. It was probably
made smaller – especially
at the right, where the
gates of Cologne were
entirely visible, as in the
print by Giovanni del Pian
(1785). The pilgrim's ships
are shown with Ursula
and the Pope
distinguishable on the first,
as they arrive in Cologne
to find that the city is
under siege by the Huns.
In the foreground a

8

warrior reads the message sent by some traitorous Roman princes warning the barbarians of their arrival. The effect of the galley that dominates the scene, a typical merchant transport ship, is truly extraordinary. The scene is taken from an engraving in the *Filocolo* by Boccaccio in the Neapolitan edition of 1475, confirmation of Carpaccio's vast knowledge of the illustrated books in his possession, and of his original ability to transpose the images.

8. *Martyrdom of the Pilgrims and the Funeral of Ursula*

Canvas, 271 × 560 cm
Acquisition: 1812,
following the Napoleonic suppressions, (cat: 580)
Latest restoration: 1984

On the base of the column is the inscription with the date 1493 and the signature: "victoris/carpatio/veneti-opus/MCCCCLXXX/XIII". The column divides the two moments of the event, and carries on it the coat of arms of the Loredan family, who commissioned the work. On the left the massacre of the pilgrims, culminating with the killing of the Pope and Ursula, who is about to be slain by an archer. A warrior witnesses the scene, powerless to help; he may be the Hun prince Julio who, according to legend, had tried in vain to save the princess. On the right the funeral of the martyrs takes place in a mausoleum bearing the inscription "ursula". The veiled woman kneeling at the foot of the catafalque could be based on Orsa (Orsola), the wife of Antonio Loredan, the hero of Scutari. It is also probable that the slaughter of the pilgrims referred to the massacres of Christian men and women perpetrated by the Turks.

9. *Apotheosis of Saint Ursula*

Canvas, 481 × 335 cm
Acquisition: 1812,
following the Napoleonic suppressions, (cat. 576)
Latest restoration: 1982-83

At the lower centre on the notice with the date of 1491 is written: "op. victoris/carpatio/MCCCCLXXXXI".
The alterpiece shows the apotheosis of Ursula, supported by a sheaf of palms held by a double crown of seraphs and flanked by two crossed standards. She is received in heaven by the Eternal Father who bestows the celestial crown upon her. Her companions, participants in the event, observe the scene, and to the left are three male figures who could be Giovanni, Marco and Jacopo, sons of Antonio Loredan. In the background, the walled and turreted city is evidently Cologne, while to the right on top of the mountain next to the lake is Scutari, defended against the Turks by Antonio Loredan himself. The ascension of Ursula is similar to an *Assumption of the Virgin*, and particularly to Mantegna's *Assumption* in the Ovetari chapel in Padua. For this work, as for the 1510 altarpiece for the Church of San Giobbe (Room 2, cat. 44), Carpaccio used two splendid preparatory drawings inspired by Perugino now kept in the Ashmolean Museum, Oxford.

21

9

A Neo-Classical Room

The arrangement of this small circular room that leads into the Sala dell'Albergo was overseen by Francesco Lazzari between 1821 and 1823, who decorated it with sculptures and bas-reliefs by Canova-influenced artists.

Rinaldo Rinaldi,
Adonis, *detail*

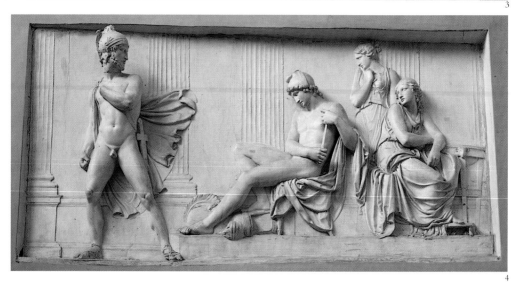

6

Rinaldo Rinaldi
(Padua, 1793-Rome, 1873)

1. *Adonis*

Marble, height 153 cm
Latest restoration: 1983

On the base to the left is the date, 1816 is enyraved. A neo-classical work, the *pendant* of the statue of the same subject in the niche in front of it.

2. *Hector Bids Farewell to Andromache*

Bas-relief, plaster, 81 × 147 cm
Latest restoration: 1983

Rinaldi, who was a student at the Venice Accademia, won the competition for admission to the Rome boarding house in April 1812. This bas-relief is the trial work sent to

Venice for his second year of study, as required by the regulations.

3. **Antonio Giaccarelli**
(Venice, 1739-Milan, 1838)

Priam Asks Achilles for the Body of Hector

Bas-relief, plaster, 96 × 180 cm
Latest restoration: 1983

Made by the artist when

he was still a student at the Accademia between 1819 and 1825.

Jacopo De Martini
(Venice 1793-1841)

4. *Hector Scolds Paris*

Bas-relief, plaster, 90 × 180 cm
Latest restoration: 1983

De Martini won the competition for an apprenticeship in Rome in 1815. Due to health problems it was difficult for him to attend, and he withdrew in 1818, before completing the training. The work was sent by him to the Accademia during his second year of study, as required by the regulations.

5. *Adonis*

Marble, height: 158 cm
Latest restoration: 1983

An academic representation of the neo-classical standards of beauty.

6. *Enone Refuses to Assist the Wounded Paris*

Bas relief, plaster, 90 × 156 cm

This group surmounted the bas-relief with Ganymede Taken by the Eagle and is a plaster copy made by De Martini of the well-known marble piece which at that time was in the Marciana library, and today is in the Archaeological Museum.

22

1

5

The former Church
of Santa Maria della Carità

The founding of the church of Santa Maria della Carità, which probably occurred at the beginning of the 12th century, is part history, part myth. According to Sansovino (1581), it was originally a small wooden building "… around a capital of an image of the Virgin, famous for various miracles." Only later was it decided to construct a church in stone on the site. In 1134 some Augustinian monks from Santa Maria in Porto relocated from Ravenna to Venice and built their convent next to the church of Santa Maria della Carità. According to legend, in 1177 Pope Alexander III – in order to escape from Federico Barbarossa – hid in the convent for six months and consecrated the church on April 5. From then on, every year on that date the Doge and Venetians of every class – even the inhabitants of the provinces – came to the church of Santa Maria della Carità to obtain the papal indulgence he had granted for the help received. Crossing the Grand Canal from Campo San Vidal to the church was made easier by the construction of a bridge of boats from Campo San Vidal to Campo Santa Maria della Carità. This custom lasted until the end of the Republic. The old façade of the church can be seen in a painting kept in Room 24, which illustrates the meeting of the Doge and the Pope. From archival documents we know that at the end of the 13th century the church had an external portico – once very common on Venetian buildings – of which there are now only two examples remaining: one at San Giacomo di Rialto and the other at San Nicolò dei Mendicoli. There was also a bell tower for this original structure, which was left intact even during the modifications made in the 15th century, until on March 17, 1744, when, due to the erosion at its base, it finally succumbed and toppled into the Grand Canal. There were many illustrious figures buried at this church as we can deduce from the register published by Tassini in 1876 – a part of this register still exists in the Seminary. The ascension of Gabriele Condulmer from the order of the Lateran Canons to the papacy (Eugene IV) in 1431, and his long pontificate, which lasted until 1447, brought new-found glory and power to the monks of La Carità. In fact, after prolonged negotiations with the members of the Scuola di Santa Maria della Carità, the monks obtained approval to enlarge the church. The new construction began in April of 1441 and was overseen by Bartolomeo Bon. Working with his son, Giovanni, Bon was responsible for all the stone work that carried the

Alvise Vivarini, Enthroned Virgin with Child and Saints, *detail*

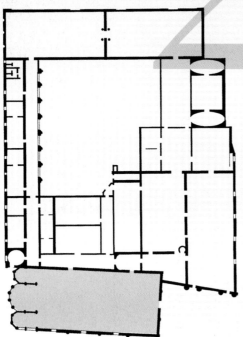

new structure: the windows, the door with the lunette above it, the side door, the round eye which was once part of the façade, the statues of *Saint Augustine*, *Saint Jerome* and the *Holy Father*, the small bell-towers, the pinnacles, the leaves on the spire of the façade (most of which are now lost), the side pillars, the ribs for the archivolts of the chapels, the cantilevers and every other decoration. At the same time, the walls were constructed in brick up to the roof, supported by fifteen beams of enormous dimensions from the region of Cadore, today still resting upon Bon's cantilevers which were completed in May of 1446, with the monogram "Ihesus". In 1450 the apse chapels were built and alongside Bartolomeo Bon this time we find "Maestro Pantaleon", who appears to have been associated with Bon in many important buildings projects in Venice at that time, including the one at Ca' d'Oro.

The decoration painted with large leaves which runs under the scarp wall of the roof and surrounds the eye on all the windows was the work of Ercole, the son of Jacobello del Fiore, who, in June of 1449, received fifty ducats for each work "... done in the Carità" and twelve more ducats on 1 December 1453 for the decoration of the chapels. As soon as building was complete, the friars decorated it with precious works of art which, with transport and customs expenses, cost a hundred ducats.. In 1453 a *Madonna* was bought from Donatello, who was sojourning in Padua at the time; the painting was placed over the door of the sacristy. Other works were commissioned from Jacopo, Gentile and Giovanni Bellini and their studio and from Cima da Conegliano. Many important funereal monuments were also erected, such as the one for the doges Marco and Agostino Barbarigo. Parts of these statues remain today and are preserved in the Franchetti Gallery at Ca' d'Oro and in the Seminary. In 1807, the whole complex of the Carità – comprising the convent, church and school – was chosen to be the site of an Academy of Fine Arts and an accompanying gallery. Begun in 1811, the modifications were headed by the architect Giannantonio Selva. The church was completely overhauled: every decoration was removed, the "barco" (low porticoed wing) and the chapels were destroyed, the Gothic windows were walled over and the entire space was divided horizontally to create five large rooms on the lower floor and two on the upper floor, with skylights, providing illumination for the exhibits. The bas-relief work by Bartolomeo Bon on the façade showing the *Coronation of the Virgin* was removed, and is now preserved in the old sacristy of the church of the Salute. From 1921 to 1923, under the direction of Gino Fogolari and with the architect Aldo Scolari, the whole space with the apses was restored including the truss ceiling and the Gothic windows on the side walls. In 1948 the room was remodelled by Carlo Scarpa. He removed large stretches of facing from the walls which imitated the original wall decoration, and placed the paintings on large larch panels covered with fabric. Out of respect for the few original architectural features remaining, the arrangement took on the appearance of a provisional exhibition space. Today the room is largely kept free to provide space for temporary shows, although some important works are on permanent display along the walls.

The right apse chapel is periodically occupied by shows of works from the Accademia's collection in storage. At the end of the 19th century the remains of stained glass windows from the second half of the 14th century were placed on the windows of the central chapel. These works once adorned the minor apses of the church of Santi Giovanni e Paolo.

Venetian school of the end of the 15th century

1. *Kneeling Angel with a Censer*

Saccharoidal marble, height: 100 cm

2. *Kneeling Angel with a Boat*

Saccharoidal marble, height: 104 cm

3. *Kneeling Angel with a Candlestick*

Saccharoidal marble, height: 106 cm

4. *Kneeling Angel with a Candlestick*

Saccharoidal marble, height: 98 cm
Acquisition: post 1849, (cat. S8, S9, S10, S11)
Latest restoration: 1980

These pieces reflect the influence of Pietro Lombardo, and were likely part of an altar or a grave monument. In August of 1849 the Fabbriceria di San Marco delivered them to the Archaeological Museum, from whence the Accademia received them.

1, 2, 3, 4

23

The Apse Triptychs
On the side walls of the apse are four triptychs that were originally in the Chiesa della Carità, on the altars of the noble chapels up against the "barco" (a structure similar to a chancel). These altars were erected between 1460 and 1464, and consecrated in 1471. Traditionally attributed to Vivarini, these triptychs were later linked to the

Bellini ambit, in particular Jacopo's studio. Records exists of drawings made in collaboration with Giovanni or rather, with Gentile and Giovanni dating the work to the late 1660's.
The archaic use of a gold background could be attributed to the use of assistants from Murano or to the wishes of the commissioners of the work. Nevertheless, the overall

form of the works, with the lunettes above, borrowed from Mantegna's altar-piece for San Zeno in Verona, must have had a great impact on Venetian artistic culture.

Jacopo Bellini, Gentile Bellini, Giovanni Bellini and collaborators

5. *Saint Lawrence between Saint John the Baptist and Saint Anthony of Paua,*

in the lunette *Madonna and Child with Angels*

Triptych
Panel, gold background
103 × 45 cm (Saints Lawrence and John the Baptist),
127 × 48 cm (Saint Anthony), 57 × 188 cm (the lunette, divided at the back into three parts)
Acquisition: 1812 (Saints Lawrence and the Baptist), following the Napoleonic suppressions, 1834 (Saint

23

5

Anthony), 1923 (the Madonna), 1954 (the two angels), from the depository of San Giovanni Evangelista from where, in 1840, they had been deposited with the Museo Correr, (cat. 621/B) Latest restoration: 1948–49

Originally on the altar of the chapel of Lorenzo Dolfin, dedicated to Saint Anthony of Padua and to Saint Stephen. The general arrangement appears influenced by Donatello, especially with regard to the three saints. Giovanni's intervention is most evident in the Madonna and Saint Lawrence.

6. *Nativity and Saints Francis and Victor* in the lunette *Trinity between Saints Domenic and Ubaldo?*

Triptych
Panels, gold background
103 × 45 cm (Nativity), 127 × 48 cm (Saints Francis and Victor), 60 × 166 cm (lunette)
Acquisition: 1834 (the saints) from the depositary of San Giovanni Evangelista, 1891 (Nativity) from Brera Collection, 1923 (the lunette), from the Correr Museum where it had been deposited, since 1840, (cat. 621) Latest restoration: 1948–49

This piece formed the altar-piece of the Natività chapel, belonging to Andrea Molin. The Trinity in the lunette is based on a drawing by Jacopo (British Museum, folio 56), while the manger scene appears to have been modelled after Vivarini models, such as the polyptych in Prague, or that of Conversano (cat. 581, in this room). The Virgin reveals the influence of Giovanni Bellini. On the back of *Saint Victor* are sketched some caricature profiles, probably by Giovanni.

23

6

Jacopo Bellini, Gentile Bellini, Giovanni Bellini and collaborators

7. Saint Sebastian between Saint John the Baptist and Saint Anthony the Abbot, in the lunette *Christ in Pietà and two angels*
Triptych

Panels, gold background
103 × 45 cm (Saint Sebastian and Saint Anthony), 127 × 48 cm

(John the Baptist), 60 × 166 cm (lunette)
Acquisition: 1821 (Saint Sebastian and Saint Anthony); 1834 (John the Baptist) from the depository of San Giovanni Evangelista; 1927 (lunette) from the Brera Picture Gallery, (cat. 621/A)

Once the altarpiece in Chapel of San Sebastiano

by Zaccaria Vitturi. It is an exact recomposition of the three panels below and they are linked together by tha landscapes. It is held to be the most significant triptych. The figure of Saint Anthony the Abbot is a strong reminder of the drawing by Giovanni Bellini in the Royal Library at Windsor, and seems to have been

inspired by *San Prosdocimo* by Donatello in the Basilica of Sant'Antonio in Padua. Not with standing the persisting gold background, the spatial articulation of the images and the chromatic beauty demonstrate an awareness of the latest in Venetian and Paduan art.

7

8. *Virgin with Child and Saint Jerome and Saint Ludovic* in the lunette *Eternity and the Annunciation* Triptych

Panels, with gold background, 127 × 48 cm (each) 59 × 170 cm (lunette)
Acquisition: 1834 (Madonna and Saints)

from the depository of San Giovanni Evangelista; 1919 (lunette) with the Austrian restitutions, (cat. 621/C) Latest restoration: 1948-49

Originally in the chapel of Sant'Orsola which, after being sold to Andrea Molin and from him to Zuane Palestrina, belonged to Giacomo Zorzi. The missing depiction of the title saint has continued to cause perplexity among critics, but was probably caused by the fact that at the first meeting with Molin, the ancona provided for five compartments, which were then reduced to only three.

8

9

10

12

11

Alvise Vivarini
(Murano 1442/43–died
between 1504 and
November 1505)

9. John the Baptist
Panel, 134 × 52 cm

10. Saint Matthew
Panel, 133 × 51 cm
Acquisition: 1812,
following the Napoleonic
suppressions, (cat. 618, 619)
Latest restoration: 1949

These two panels –
damaged at the top –
were originally in the
church of San Pietro
Martire on Murano. They
are probably the remnants
of a polyptych, and date
to just after the *Madonna
with Saints* (Room 23,
cat. 607) of 1480. The
bare landscape at the feet
of the saints, particularly
of John the Baptist, is
particularly suggestive.

11. Nicolò di Pietro,
ascribed to.
(documented in Venice
from 1394 to 1430)
The Arrival of the Magi
Panel, 58 × 93 cm
Acquisition: 1816,
bequest from Girolamo
Molin, (cat. 12)
Latest restoration: 1995

Analysis of the work was
confounded during the
19th century by the
signature of Guariento,
which was only called into
doubt at the end of the
century. The most recent
restoration has brought to
light the original vivid
colours and exquisite
elegance, and would seem
to confirm the attribution
of the painting to Nicolò
di Pietro.

**12. Nicola di Maestro
Antonio di Ancona**
(active from 1460 to c. 1485)
Crucifixion
Panel, 101 × 70 cm

Acquisition: 1816,
bequest from Girolamo
Molin, (cat. 51)
Latest restoration: 1985

This painting has been
attributed to a long and
varied series of artists, all
in the Padua area, until it
was recognised as an early
work of the Ancona
master. It probably dates
to around the early
1470s, given the
deformation brought on
by the Mantegna-inspired
predella of San Zeno.

13. Gentile Bellini
(Venice 1429-1507)

*The Blessed Lorenzo
Giustiniani*

Canvas, 221 × 155 cm
Acquisition: 1852, from the
Church of Madonna
dell'Orto, (cat. 570)
Latest restoration: 1965

On the inscription at the
lower centre is the date
1455 and the signature.
From the church of
Madonna dell'Orto, this
painting was displayed
only in 1887. It may have
originally been a
processional standard,
which would explain the
poor condition of the
work and is the first
dated piece by Gentile
Bellini, painted nine years
after the death of the first
patriarch of Venice.
Analysis of the profile of
the ascetic, while further
pointing to the influence
of Andrea Mantegna, also
reveals the artist's knack
for objective painting, an
ability which will
eventually lead to his
appointment as the
official painter of the
Signoria.

23

13

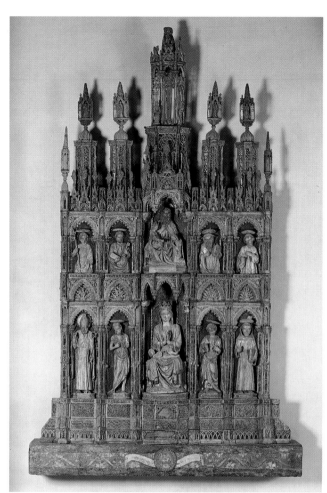

14. **Bartolomeo Giolfino**
(Verona c. 1410-c.1486)

Madonna Enthroned with Child and Three Saints, and the Coronation of the Virgin with Saints

Sculpted and painted wood, 380 × 187 cm
Acquisition: 1909, by purchase, (cat. S2)
Latest restoration: 1980

On the scroll on the base is the fragmented inscription with the signature and the date of 1470. From the oratory of the Querini palazzo in Pressano (near Verona), with the Querini coat of arms on the base itself. The work has lost much of its original colour, but the carving work – also fragmentary by now – is a highly refined example of Gothic style.

15. **Maestro della Madonna del Parto**

The Madonna del Parto and Two Devotees

Panel, 188 × 138 cm
Acquisition: 1916, on deposit from the Church of Santa Caterina, (cat. 1328)
Latest restoration: 1996

On the open book is an invocation to the Virgin Mary, Madonna del Parto. The work is from

14

16

the late 14th century and comes from the church of Santa Caterina. Similar to early works by Nicolò di Pietro, this work was probably painted in Venice, although it was previously attributed to an Emilian artist.

16. **Bartolomeo Vivarini**
(Venice c. 1430–records up until 1491)

Madonna Enthroned with sleeping Child and Saints Andrew, John the Battista, Domenico and Peter

Panels, gold background, 131 × 49 cm, 107 × 33 cm
Acquisition: 1812, following the Napoleonic suppressions, (cat. 615)

Latest restoration: 1994

In the centre compartment toward the bottom is the signature and date of 1454. The polyptych comes from the church of S. Andrea on the island of Certosa, where it was placed at the altar of the Ca' Morosini chapel. An engraving by G. Sasso

provides testimony of the now lost frame with a *Crucifixion* engraved among the half-figures of prophets. This is one of the most important works by the artist; the *Virgin with Child* will be alluded to by Giovanni Bellini in his *Madonna Enthroned* (Room 4, cat. 591).

23

15

17   18   20   21

Alvise Vivarini
(Murano 1442/43–died
between 1504 and
November 1505)

17. *Beatified Martyr*
Panel, 143 × 40 cm
Acquisition: 1919, with
the Austrian restitutions,
(cat. 593/A)

18. *Saint Claire*
Panel, 144 × 38 cm
Acquisition: 1828,
following the Napoleonic
suppressions, (cat. 593)
Latest restoration: 1948
Recorded by Boschini
(1664) in the church of San
Daniele, originally used by

Benedictine nuns, and from
1437 by Augustinian nuns.
Chiara Ogniben Sustan was
responsible for the change
of order; the
psychologically charged
face of Saint Claire (Chiara)
has led some critics to
suggest that this may be a

portrait of Chiara Ogniben
Sustan. The position of the
green curtains on the two
panels implies that they
were two independent
works and not part of a
larger piece. The works date
from 1485-1490.

19. *Madonna Enthroned*
Panel, 175 × 196 cm
Acquisition: 1812,
following the Napoleonic
suppressions, (cat. 607)
Latest restoration: 1993

On the base of the throne is
the date 1480 and the
signature. The work was
originally on the altar of
Santa Maria della Prà, and
then on the altar of San
Bernardino in the church of
San Francesco in Treviso,
which the minor friars
beautified with works by
Venetian artists – including
Giovanni Mansueti and
Carpaccio – over the 15th
and 16th centuries
(Quadreria cat. 97 and 90).
The work is a masterpiece:
the green curtain behind,
while still quite old, was
added at a later date and is
of a material that x-ray
analyses have not been able
to penetrate. The
composition must have
originally been arranged

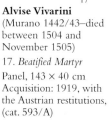

19

with the windows opening on to the landscape, as in the *Virgin Adoring the Sleeping Baby Jesus* in the church of San Giovanni in Bragora. The bust of Saint Anthony also appears on a panel in the Museo Correr.

Bartolomeo Vivarini
(c. 1430–records until 1491)

20. Saint Mary Magdalene

Panel, 132 × 48 cm

21. Saint Barbara

Panel, 132 × 48 cm
Acquisition: 1812, following the Napoleonic suppressions, (cat. 584, 585)
Latest restoration: 1979

The signature and date (1490) appear on the scroll on the lower part of Saint Barbara. These two works come from the now destroyed church of San Geminiano in Venice. They are from the later period of the artist's life, and present a monumentality that foreshadows the next century.

22. Saint Ambrose Blessing the Devotees, with Saints Louis, Peter, Paul and Sebastian

Panel, gold background, 125 × 47 cm (central), 108 × 36 cm (sides)
Acquisition: 1919, with the Austrian restitutions, (cat. 825)
Latest restoration: 1997

On the lower part of Saint Peter are the signature and date (1477); on the lower part of Saint Paul is the

23

signature of the creator of the lost frame: Giacomo da Faenza. This polyptych comes from the Tagliapietra Confraternity, and was probably a devotional piece donated by some members and dedicated to their personal saints, as the writing under Saint Ambrose would indicate. The work has a surprisingly impressionist effect, with a similarly strong use of colour.

23. **Lazzaro Bastiani**
(Venice, 1425/30–c. 1512)

Nativity Scene with Saints James, Eustacius, Nicholas and Mark

Panel, 160 × 191 cm
Acquisition: 1812, following the Napoleonic suppressions, (cat. 100)
Latest restoration: 1994

Originally in the church of Sant'Elena. The painting was completed according to the

will of Eustachio Balbi, who died in 1480. The design of the dwelling seems inspired by similar dwellings painted by Jacopo Bellini in the books of drawings in the Louvre and the British Museum. The unusual format of the piece is similar to the *Virgin and Saints* by Alvise Vivarini (Room 23, cat. 607), dating from 1480. The artist's illusionistic ability to create extreme depth through the structure of the dwelling is impressive.

23

22a   22b   22c   22d   22e

24. **Andrea da Murano**
(records from 1463 to 1504)

Saints Vincent Ferreri and Roch, with Saint Sebastian and Saint Peter the Martyr, Madonna della Misericordia with Saints Louis (?), Dominic, Thomas Aquinas and Catherine of Siena

Canvas transferred from a panel, 152 × 88 cm (central panel); panel, 152 × 47 cm (sides); panel, 80 × 199 cm (lunette)
Acquisition: the pieces of the work, which was returned after the Napoleonic suppressions, were united in 1883, (cat. 28)
Latest restoration: 1948

Signed at the lower centre, this triptych was originally in the church of San Pietro Martire on Murano. All of the saints represented on the lower order – including Saint Peter, after whom the church was named – are venerated for their magical qualities against the plague; Saint Roch indicates a bubo under his clothing, while the small devotees and commissioners kneeling seem to be praying for protection against contagion. The artist was an attentive observer of

24

the artistic trends developing in those years in the area of the Venetian lagoon, and was among the few Venetians who truly understood the work of Andrea del Castagno. The work was surely painted in relation to a plague, probably the one of 1478.

Carlo Crivelli
(Venice, 1430/35–died between August 7, 1494, and September, 1495)
25. *Saints Peter and Paul*
Panel, 217 × 72 cm
26. *Saints Jerome and Augustine*
Panel, 217 × 72 cm
Acquisition: 1883 (Saints Jerome and Augustine); 1895, (Saints Peter and Paul) by purchase, (cat. 103, 103/A)
Latest restoration: 1979

Originally in the Cathedral of Camerino, where they were located alongside the *Madonna della Candeletta*. The church was destroyed by an earthquake in 1799, and the *Madonna* and *Saints Jerome and Augustine* were taken to the Brera gallery in Milan; they were transferred to the Accademia in 1883. The panel with *Saints Peter and Paul* was recovered from under the rubble and sold to the State. In spite of the fact that the expressionism of the saints seems to be in contrast with the formal elegance of the Madonna, the pieces were part of a single complex, as is shown by the similar dimensions and the repetition of the identical parapet. As the central panel is signed with the title of *eques*, an honour bestowed upon the painter in 1490 by prince Ferdinando of Capua, the paintings should correspond to around that date.

27. **Bartolomeo Vivarini**
and workshop
(c. 1430–records until 1491)
Conversano Polyptych
Panels, 154 × 46 cm (central), 138 × 23 cm (sides), 25 × 270 cm (predella), 46 × 45 cm (cyma)
Acquisition: 1883, by purchase from the Conversano Duomo, (cat. 581)
Latest restoration: 1995

On the central panel is shown the Nativity scene, with Saints Francis, Andrew, John the Baptist, Peter, Paul, Jerome, Dominic and Theodore. Below in the Nativity scene is an inscription with the date (1475), while on the listel of the predella frame is another with the signature. The fact that the work was to be sent to Apulia made it a less binding undertaking for the artist. Although the central group translates the one made by Antonio Vivarini for a 1447 polyptych into more substantial and animated forms, the saints at the sides and the predella seem weaker and not to have been painted by the artist himself.

25

26

27

Canvases from the Sala dell'Albergo of the Scuola Grande di San Marco.

The five canvases located at the back of the church, together with the *Sermon of Saint Mark at Alexandria* by Gentile Bellini and the *Baptism of Saint Mark* by Giovanni Mansueti – today in the Brera Museum – were part of the original decoration of the Albergo Room of the Scuola di San Marco. In 1492 Gentile and Giovanni Bellini offered to paint the room, and came to an agreement with the Scuola. However, Gentile died in 1507 without finishing the *Sermon*, which was completed by Giovanni. In 1515 the Scuola hired Giovanni to paint the *Martyrdom of Saint Mark*, but unfortunately on November 29, 1516, the artist died and the work was left unfinished until Vittore Belliniano completed it in 1526. Later works were commissioned from Giovanni Mansueti, collaborator and disciple of Gentile Bellini, thus guaranteeing the stylistic continuity of the cycle. Mansueti died in 1526 or 1527, and the last two paintings, *The Presentation of Saint Mark's Ring* by Paris Bordon, and the *Sea Storm (Burrasca di mare)* by Palma il Vecchio, reveal a radical change in the taste of the commissioners. When the Scuola was suppressed by Napoleonic decree in 1806, the cycle was dispersed, with pieces in Milan, Venice and Vienna. The works in Vienna were returned in 1919 and the cycle was re-assembled at the Accademia Galleries in 1994 (but without the paintings in the Brera Museum).

23

2

1. Giovanni Bellini
(1434/39–1516) and
Vittore Belliniano
(records from 1507 to 1529)

Martyrdom of Saint Mark

Canvas, 362 × 771 cm,
the central cut at door
level is 158 × 172 cm
Acquisition: 1919, with
the Austrian restitutions,
(cat. 1002)
Latest restoration: 1987-94

On July 4th, 1515, the
Scuola commissioned
Giovanni Bellini to paint
a canvas with the story of
Saint Mark, who "... in
Alexandria was dragged
along the ground by
those infidel Moors".
This is the scene of the
martyrdom that appears
in the Marciani mosaics:
during the Easter feast
Mark's adversaries had
sent soldiers to arrest the
saint; dragging him by a
cord tied around his neck
they went through the
streets of Alexandria for
the entire day and until
the next morning when

he died. The paintings in
the Doge's Palace have
been lost, so this is one of
the very rare examples of
the artist's larger
decorative works,
although it was not
painted entirely by him.
In fact, when Giovanni
died on November 19,
1516, the work was
completed by Vittore
Belliniano, Bellini's co-
worker in the Doge's
Palace, who placed his
signature on it and the
date of 1526; ten years
later. The drawing and
preparation of the great
canvas are doubtless the
work of Giovanni based
on a sketch by his
brother, but the actual
painting on the canvas
was by Vittore. Perhaps, as
recent critics have
proposed, he also had the
collaboration of Lorenzo
Lotto, who was a guest of
the convent of Santi
Giovanni e Paolo,
attached to the Scuola di
San Marco, from 1525 to

1526. But it is clear that
Bellini was responsible
for the view with San
Ciriaco of Ancona in the
background on the hill,
which is similar to the
one that appears on
Nicolini's *Crucifixion*
which is now in Prato.

2. Giovanni Mansueti
(records from 1485–died
between September,
1526, and March, 1527)

Saint Mark Heals Aniano

Canvas, 370 × 407 cm
Acquisition: 1838 (cat. 569)
Latest restoration: 1992-94

This painting and the
Baptism of Aniano, today
in the Brera Gallery
surely refer to the "doi
telleri in albergo" (the
two canvases in the Sala
dell'Albergo) that the
Scuola decided to have
painted on October 24,
1518. Gentile Bellini died
in 1507, Giovanni in
1516, and Vittore
Belliniano was still
occupied on his

Martyrdom so Mansueti, a
disciple primarily of
Gentile, whose drawings
he had worked on, with
his somewhat behind-
the-times taste must have
seemed a logical choice
to guarantee the stylistic
unity of the cycle. The
Guardian Grande
Antonio de Maistri
commissioned the piece,
assigning the third canvas
to Mansueti in 1525,
presumably the year
when the two paintings
were completed. This
painting was to left
(Room 23, cat. 516), after
the *Sea-Storm* and the
*Presentation of Saint Marks
Ring* (Room 23, cat.
320). It depicts an
episode in the life of
Saint Mark. When he
reache Alexandria, he
breaks a strap on his
sandal and the archangel
Michael appears to him
and has Mark follow him
so he can show Mark his
successor. Mark finds the
cobbler Aniano and gives
the sandal to him. While
Aniano is repairing the
sandal, he injures his left
hand, which Mark heals
with his saliva mixed
with dust from the street.
The scene takes place
within an interesting
architectural context; the
building at the back with
the veiled women recalls
the *Prayer*, now in the
Brera gallery, and the
descriptions of Vasari of a
lost painting by Alvise
Vivarini in the Sala del
Maggior Consiglio; the
decorations of this Sala
were the inspiration for
the entire cycle in the
Albergo. An inscription at
the centre describes the
miracle, while to the
lower left a camel driver
holds a scroll with the
artist's signature.

1

3. **Giovanni Mansueti**
(records from 1485–died
between September, 1526
and March, 1527)

*Episodes from the Life of
Saint Mark*

Canvas, 371 × 603 cm
Acquisition: 1838,
following the Napoleonic

suppressions, (cat. 562)
Latest restoration: 1992-94

To the lower left, a baby
holds a scroll with the
artist's signature. This work
was originally in the Sala
dell'Albergo between the
two windows, and was
commissioned by the

Guardian Grande Antonio
di Maistri in 1525. When
Mansueti was dying,
between September 1526
and March 1527, the
painting was nearly
finished, although "some
heads" had not yet been
added. The composition is
articulated in three

23

episodes. To the right, under a loggia, the idolatrous Egyptians plot against Mark, envious of his ever-growing number of followers. At the centre, the saint is beset by enemies while celebrating mass and they then drag him through the streets of Alexandria. To the left, he is brought into jail, where an angel appears to him to announce his entrance into a new life. At this announcement Mark thanks Jesus and prays for him to receive his soul, at which point Jesus appears to him and speaks the famous words "Pax tibi, Marce, evangelista meus" ("Peace be with you, Mark, my Evangelist"). According to the affirmations of his daughter Cecilia, Mansueti included the portraits of the more important members of the Scuola in the painting.

23

3

4. **Jacopo Palma il Vecchio**

(Serina, Bergamo, c. 1480–Venice 1528) and

Paris Bordon

(Treviso 1500–Venice 1571)

Sea Storm

Canvas, 362 × 408 cm
Acquisition: 1829,
following the Napoleonic
suppressions, (cat. 516)
Latest restoration: 1993-94

This work was originally in the Sala dell'Albergo, immediately to the left after entering. The work was almost certainly referred to by the Scuola on November 5, 1534, when the room was described as decorated "with paintings", including "the painting that will be delivered in a few days". It must have remained unfinished or in some way damaged after its completion, as the large insert to the right with the boat containing the fisherman and the three saints would attest; this part has been attributed to Paris Bordon. Before displaying it at the Accademia Galleries in 1830, the part to the lower left with the John Dory was also added by Sebastiano Santi in order to fill in the missing part corresponding to a doorway. This painting and the following one depict the legend of a terrible storm with very high seas that occurred on the night of February 25, 1341. An old fisherman found shelter under a bridge in the place that was then called Terranova, where the public granaries were located and where the formerly royal gardens are now. A man came to the fisherman from the nearby church of San Marco, and asked the fisherman to take him to the island of San Giorgio, where another stranger also boarded the boat. They then went towards San Nicolò del Lido, where a third person came aboard. While the storm raged on, Saint Mark, Saint George and Saint Nicholas all appeared to the fisherman. Suddenly a large galley containing countless devils appeared in the churning sea before them and headed towards Venice to destroy the city. The three angels intervened and sent the ship to the bottom of the sea. Before returning into his church as the other saints had done, Mark gave the astonished fisherman a ring to give to the Doge as proof of the events he had witnessed.

The sailboat at the centre was inspired by a drawing by Lorenzo Lotto for one of the inlaid wood pieces of Santa Maria Maggiore in Bergamo. The authorship of the painting, whose identification was always problematic, has been

4

made difficult by the many changes and additions made to the piece. In 1550 Vasari attributed it to Giorgione, but in the 1568 edition he attributed it to Palma. It is probable that after the death of Mansueti between 1527 and 1528, the painting was indeed entrusted to Palma, who was a member of the Scuola from 1513 until his death on July 30, 1528. The work was probably commissioned in the years immediately prior to this date, and so he may not have had the time to finish the canvas, which instead was completed or repaired by Paris Bordon in 1534.

5. **Paris Bordon**
(Treviso 1500–Venice 1571)
Presentation of Saint Mark's Ring

Canvas by transposition from another canvas, 370 × 300 cm
Acquisition: 1815, following the Napoleonic suppressions, with the restitutions from Paris, (cat. 320)
Latest restoration: 1988

This work was originally in the Sala dell'Albergo, on the left between *Sea Storm* and *Saint Mark Heals Aniano*. The work is related to the Scuola's decision on January 12, 1534 to have made "uno o doi teleri" ("one or two paintings"), for which a competition was held. On the base of the pillar at right is the signature. The work shows the fisherman who offers the ring of Saint Mark – which tradition still holds as being among the treasures of the Basilica – to the Doge as proof of the miraculous events of the night before. Surrounding Doge Andrea Gritti (1522-38) are the senators, while on the left is the Great Guardian and a group of members of the confraternity. The complex architectural setting of the background – suggestive of the Doge's Palace – was inspired by Sebastiano Serlio. The decision of 1534 notwithstanding, this painting, which was enthusiastically praised by Vasari, dates to the early 1540s, as is evidenced by its adhesion to the teachings of Titian and of the Tuscan artists in Venice at that time.

5

The former Sala dell'Albergo
of the Scuola di Santa Maria della Carità

This was the main room of the Scuola di Santa Maria della Carità, where the most high ranking members met, and where the registers, charters (called the "mariegola"), and the relics were all kept. The ceiling, gilt and multicoloured, with the four *Evangelists*, dates from the end of the 15th century. The *Holy Father* at the centre was probably taken from a previous ceiling in the Chapter Hall which may have been destroyed by fire. In 1811 Selva opened the short stairway; for this occasion the wooden altar was disassembled and the triptych by Antonio Vivarini and Giovanni d'Alemagna was moved to the right wall.

Tiziano Vecellio,
Presentation of Mary in
the Temple, *detail*

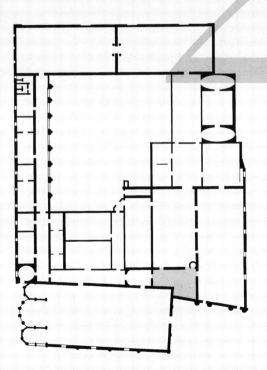

1. Antonio Vivarini
(c. 1418/20-1476/84) and
Giovanni d'Alemagna
(records from 1441-1450)

*The Virgin Enthroned with
Saints Gregory, Jerome,
Ambrose and Augustine.*

Canvases
344 × 203 cm (central),
344 × 137 cm (sides)
Acquisition: 1807,
following the Napoleonic
suppressions, (cat. 625)
Latest restoration: in
progress

On the step of the throne
is written the date 1446
and the signature. This
work was painted for the
Sala dell'Albergo, for the
wall opposite Titian's
Presentation, where a
wooden frame was
inserted which was
destroyed along with the
altar in 1811, when the
connecting access was
opened. One of the
oldest Venetian paintings
on canvas, it is certainly
the most unified work
the two artists produced
in their problematic
collaboration. The Virgin
and angels are clearly
attributable to Vivarini.
The new notions about
perspective are evident in
spite of the abundance of
decoration, which must
have appeared even more
opulent when framed and
with the pastel ornaments
on the saints' copes, now
lost. These notions
probably reflect the
artists' awareness of the
graphic studies Donatello
made in preparation for
the Santo altar in Padua.

24

2. **Titian**
(Tiziano Vecellio)
(Pieve di Cadore c. 1480/90–Venice 1576)

Presentation of the Virgin

Canvas, 335 × 775 cm
Acquisition: 1807, following the Napoleonic suppressions, (cat. 626)
Latest restoration: 1981

This large canvas was painted for the Sala dell'Albergo of the Scuola della Carità between August 21, 1534 and March 6, 1539. In addition to this work, the walls of the room were also decorated to the left by the *Marriage of the Virgin* by Giampietro Silvio, and to the right by Girolamo Dente's *Annunciation*, still in storage at the parish of Mason Vicentino. The painting appears to have been cut at the bottom to accommodate the two doors. The door to the observer's right already existed and was probably the Gothic doorway, today walled over, which was the old entrance of the ground floor room. The left-hand door was opened on March 10, 1572, while Titian was still alive, and required the sacrifice of part of the painting. Although the horizontal course of the wall incorporates a certain approach to design taken from the Venetian narrative tradition – and mostly from Carpaccio – it does so with an extraordinarily 'modern' spirit and a deep awareness of contemporary architectural notions proposed by Sansovino and Serlio. The perfect balance between architecture and landscape, and between these two and the open procession of the members of the confraternity, firmly establishes the unity of the work; a new interpretation of the 15th century models and of great importance for the painters who followed.

24

2

3

4

3. Veneto–Byzantine School of the 14th and 15th Centuries

Reliquary of Cardinal Bessarione

Wood, silver, gilt filigree, enamel, glass and precious stones, 47 × 32 cm
Acquisition: 1919, with the suppression of the Scuola, it first entered the collection of Luigi Savorgnan and later that of Abbot Luigi Celotti, who sold it to the Emperor Francis I in 1821. Assigned to the Galleries with the Austrian restitutions, (cat. S19)

Donated to the Scuola della Carità in 1463 by Cardinal Bessarione, the famous scholar who with the bequest of his manuscripts brought about the institution of the Marciana library. This piece, which even Gentile Bellini helped to construct, was originally located in a tabernacle (now dispersed) on the altar on the wall where now the short stairway begins. The precious piece is formed of a cross with Christ encased on an enamelled tablet which includes four rock crystal cases containing the "Holy Wood" and "Holy Shroud" relics, two plates with the archangels Gabriel and Michael, Constantine and Saint Helena painted on glass, a cover composed of a fixed part framing the reliquary on three sides with seven small scenes from *The Passion* and a moveable shutter cover on which the Crucifixion is depicted. The origin and date of the rare and complex work is problematic, not only because of the difficulty of interpreting the Greek and Latin inscriptions, but also because the embedding for the cross and the painted cover are probably the work of Bessarione.

4. Anonymous 16th century Veneto artist

Portrait of Cardinal Bessarione

Canvas, 116 × 95 cm
Acquisition: 1807, following the Napoleonic suppressions, (cat. 876)

Originally in the Sala dell'Albergo, this painting was commissioned by the Scuola della Carità on March 8, 1540. Cardinal Bessarione is depicted holding the reliquary given to him by the Scuola itself and wearing the apparel of a member of the confraternity.

5. Venetian School 16th Century

Doge Ziani Meets Pope Alexander III at the Chiesa della Carità

Canvas, 185 × 234 cm
Acquisition: 1884, from the Doge's Palace, (cat. 654)

This painting may originally have been in the Carità church. It depicts Doge Ziani meeting Pope Alexander III. According to legend, the pope had come to Venice while fleeing Barbarossa. The piece is also interesting for documentary reasons, as it shows how the façade of the church and the Scuola appeared in the 16th century.

24

5

The "Quadreria" Gallery

In the early seventies on the top floor of the Palladian Monastery, the Accademia Galleries were provided with a repository created with two aims in mind: a secondary gallery in the long corridor, well in keeping with the existing building, and a room for consultation in a spacious enclosed environment, with the paintings arranged on fixed metal trellises. The long, elegant corridor was conceived by Andrea Palladio as an entranceway to the cells of the large religious order, the Lateran canons for whom he had "tried to make this abode like that of the Ancients'". Access to it is afforded from the oval stairway of which the architect himself wrote: "I made of it an empty place in the middle of the *Monastero della Carità* in Venice that is truly admirable". Indeed, as he had predicted in his treatise, "when standing atop the stairway, one can see – and be seen by – everyone who ascends or begins to ascend".

These structural works belonging now to the distant past, both the stairway and corridor were in need of full restoration, and the paintings required a more fitting position. By fortuitous coincidence, the restoration works of 1995 were undertaken at almost the same time as the restoration of the terracotta façade, dated 1561, and of the *tablinum*, which in the house of the ancients was the space dedicated to the Penates or household gods and used as a vestry, and which today belongs to the Academy of Fine Arts.

The long corridor has been conceived as a type of storeroom, which is organised chronologically with suitable lighting and fittings. Here, about 80 paintings are found and can be viewed not just by scholars but also by all visitors, upon prior booking.

Nicolò di Pietro
(recorded in Venice from 1394 to 1430)

The Virgin with Child with Saint Martha and Saint Catherine

Canvas, 104 × 139 cm
Acquisition: 1960, from the state depository, (cat. 1237)
Latest restoration: 1995

Marco Antonio di Ruggero known as 'Marco Zoppo'
(Cento 1453-Venice 1478)
Master of the Cattaver
(active in Venice between 1460 and c. 1470)

Christ Blessing with Saints Vincenzo Ferreri, Augustine, Helen and Francis

Canvas, 136 × 407 cm
Acquisition: 1838, following the Napoleonic suppressions, (cat. 614, 622, 620)
Latest restoration: 1984-87

Lazzaro Bastiani
(Venice c. 1425/30 -1512)

Saint Anthony in the Nut-Tree

Arched panel, 234 × 140 cm
Acquisition: 1862, following the Napoleonic suppression, (cat. 104)

Saint Veneranda Enthroned

Arched panel, 325 × 217 cm
Acquisition: 1919, with the Austrian restitutions, (cat. 822)
Latest restoration: 1995

Gerolamo da Treviso il Vecchio
(Gerolamo di Bartolomeo Strazzaroli di Aviano, 1451-1497)

The Virgin Enthroned with a Franciscan Bishop (Louis?) and Saints Anthony, Francis and Prosdocimo (or Basil)

Panel, 208 × 214 cm
Acquisition: 1915-18, spoils of war, (cat. 886)
Latest restoration: 1985-1995

The Transfiguration

Panel in the shape of a lunette, 172 × 263 cm
Acqustion: 1812, following the Napoleonic suppressions, (cat. 96)

Pier Maria Pennacchi
(Treviso 1464-1514/15)

Death of the Virgin

Panel, 134 × 168 cm
Acquisition: 1907, by purchase, (cat. 657)
Latest restoration: 1995

Giovanni Buonconsiglio, known as 'Marescalco'
(Montecchio Maggiore, Vicenza? c. 1465-1536/37)

Saint Benedict, Saint Thecla and Saint Damian

Panel, 82 × 68 cm
Acquisition: 1856, by purchase the Manfrin Collection, (cat. 602)
Latest restoration: 1958

Giovanni Bellini and assistants
(1434/39-1516)

Saint Peter

Canvas, 224 × 105 cm
Acquisition: 1898, from the state depository, (cat. 734)
Latest restoration: 1995

Nicolò Rondinelli
(recorded from 1495 to 1502)

The Virgin and Child with Saint Jerome

Panel, 82 × 59 cm
Acquisition: 1917, by purchase, (cat. 904)
Latest restoration: 1995

Giovanni Mansueti
(records from 1485-died between September 1526 and March 1527)

Saint Sebastian with Saints Liberale, Gregory, Francis and Roch

Panel, 203 × 201 cm
Acquisition: 1810, following the Napoleonic suppressions, (cat. 97)
Latest restoration 1995

Giovanni Agostino da Lodi
(active 1490s, with records up to c. 1520)

Virgin and Child with Saint Simon and Saint Jerome

Panel, 71 × 111 cm
Acquisition: 1838, following the Napoleonic suppressions, (cat. 605)
Latest restoration: 1990

Francesco Morone
(Verona 1471-1529)

The Virgin and Child

Canvas, 72 × 54 cm
Acquisition: 1932, by purchase from Giovanelli collection, (cat. 916)

Bartolomeo Cincani, known as Montagna
(Vicenza c. 1449 - 11 October, 1523)

The Virgin and Child Entrhoned with Saint Sebastian and Saint Jerome

Panel,
215 × 162 cm
Acquisition: 1816, bequest of Girolamo Molin, (cat. 80)
Latest restoration: 1994-95

Giambattista Cima da Conegliano
(Conegliano 1459-1517)

The Archangel Raphael and Tobias with Saint Nicholas and Saint James the Great

Canvas transferred from panel, 162 × 178 cm
Acquisition: 1888, by purchase, (cat. 592)

Giambattista Cima da Conegliano, workshop of
(Conegliano 1459-1517)

Saint Mark Enthroned with Saint Andrew and Saint Louis

Canvas, 222 × 341 cm (cat. 816)

Justice

Canvas, 189 × 80 cm (cat. 165)

Temperance

Canvas, 189 × 85 cm (cat. 167)
Acquisition: 1838, the two lateral figures following the Napoleonic suppressions; 1919, the central section with the Austrian restitutions
Latest restoration: 1959

Vittore Carpaccio
(Venice? c. 1460-1525/26)

Meeting of Joachim and Anne, with Saint Louis IX and Saint Libera

Panel, 186 × 169 cm
Acquisition: 1812, following the Napoleonic suppressions, (cat. 90)
Latest restoration: 1982-95

Francesco Bissolo
(c. 1475-1554)

The Presentation of Christ to Simeon with Saints and the Donor

Panel, 80 × 119 cm
Acquisition: 1950, bequest of Felicita Renier, (cat. 93)
Latest restoration: 1995

Lorenzo Luzzo
(documented from 1511 to 1526)

The Virgin and Child with Saint Vitus, Saint Modesto and Christ the Redeemer in Glory

Canvas, 187 × 120 cm
Acquisition: 1926, by purchase, (cat. 814)
Latest restoration: 1988

Marco Basaiti
(Venice 1470/75–post 1530)

Saint George and the Princess

Canvas, 229 × 156 cm
Acquisition: 1899, by purchase,
(cat. 102)
Latest restoration: 1994

Marco Basaiti?
(Venice 1470/75–post 1530)

Portrait of a Man

Panel, 31 × 23 cm
Acquisition: 1900 by purchase
(cat. 645)
Latest restoration: 1995

**Veneto School of the Second
decade of the 16th century**

Christ with the Doctors

Panel, 152 × 176 cm
Acquisition: 1816, bequest of
Girolamo Molin, (cat. 85)
Latest restoration: 1995

**Benedetto Rusconi,
known as 'Diana'**
(Venice c. 1460–1525)

*The Virgin and Child with Saints
Jerome, Benedict, Mary Magdalene
and Justina*

Panel, 200 × 230 cm
Acquisition: 1812, following the
Napoleonic suppressions, (cat. 82)
Latest restoration: 1995

Giovanni Francesco Caroto
(Verona c. 1480–1555)

The Madonna Sewing

Canvas, 59 × 47 cm
Acquisition: 1889, by purchase,
(cat. 609)
Latest restoration: 1995

Rocco Marconi
(Treviso c. 1470/75–recorded in
Venice from 1504, died before 13
May, 1529)

*Christ with Saint John the Baptist and
Saint Peter*

Canvas, 185 × 124 cm
Acquisition: 1812, following the
Napoleonic suppressions (cat. 317)
Latest restoration: 1957-58

Sebastiano Florigerio
(Conegliano? c. 1500/05–died after
1550 and before December 29,
1564)

The Virgin and Child with Saint Anne

between Saint Roch and Saint
Sebastian (in the lunette)
*Saint John the Evangelist with Saint
Anthony of Padua and Saint Francis*
also called *The Immaculate
Conception Altarpiece*

Panel, 240 × 181 cm (lower
section), 94 × 185 cm (lunette)
Acquisition: 1829, following the
Napoleonic suppressions, (cat. 157)
Latest restoration: 1995

**Jacopo Negretti known as
Palma il Vecchio** and workshop
(Serina, Bergamo c. 1480–Venice
1528)

Christ and the Woman of Canaan

Panel, 95 × 155 cm
Acquisition: 1838, donated by
Girolamo Contarini, (cat.310)
Latest restoration: 1995

Titian and workshop
(c. 1480/90–1576)

Symbol of Saint Luke (Bull)

Panel, 455 × 2360 cm (cat.1035a)

Symbol of Saint Matthew (Angel)

Panel, 495 × 2030 cm (cat. 1035b)

Symbol of Saint Mark (Lion)

Panel, 455 × 2400 cm (cat. 1035c)

Symbol of Saint John (Eagle)

Panel, 495 × 1980 cm (cat. 1035d)

Cherub Head

Panel, 45 × 40 cm (cat. 1035m)

Two Cherub Heads

Panel, 40,5 × 46,5 cm (cat. 1035t)

Mask of Satyr

Panel, 59 × 58 cm (cat. 1035h)

Face of a Woman

Panel, 49 × 43 cm (cat.1035o)
Acquisition: 1812, following the
Napoleonic suppressions
Latest restoration: 1989

Paris Bordon
(Treviso 1500–Venice 1571)

Winged Putti with Garlands

Panel, 52 × 101 cm
Acquisition: 1816,
donated by Girolamo Molin, (cat. 311)
Latest restoration: 1980

**Bonifacio de' Pitati
known as Bonifacio Veronese**
(Verona 1487–Venice 1553)

Christ and the Apostles

Panel, 189 × 151 cm
Acquisition: 1814, following the
Napoleonic suppressions, (cat. 309)
Latest restoration: 1955

The Visiting Angel

Canvas, 198 × 135 cm
Acquisition: 1919, with the
Austrian restitutions, (cat. 942)

The Virgin

Canvas, 197 × 137 cm
Acquisition: 1919, with the
Austrian restitutions, (cat. 943)
Latest restoration: 1963

**Andrea Meldolla,
known as Schiavone**
(Zadar c. 1510/15–Venice 1563)

Christ before Pilate

Canvas, 104 × 170 cm
Acquisition: 1850, bequest
of Felicita Renier, (cat. 271)
Latest restoration: 1956

**Jacopo Robusti,
known as Tintoretto**
(Venice 1519–1594)

The Crucifixions on Mount Ararat

Incomplete panel, 138 × 218 cm
Acquisition: 1865, following the
Napoleonic suppressions, (cat. 1091)
Latest restoration: 1960

Saint Peter

Canvas, 104 × 33 cm
Acquisition: 1838, donated by
Girolamo Contarini, (cat. 506)
Latest restoration: 1960

Saint Paul

Canvas, 104 × 33 cm
Acquisition: 1838, donated by
Girolamo Contarini, (cat. 501)
Latest restoration: 1960

The Presentation of Christ at the Temple

Canvas, 237 × 296 cm
Acquisition: 1960, by decree, (cat. 725)
Latest restoration: 1986

The Deposition

Canvas, 227 × 294 cm
Acquisition: 1806, following the
Napoleonic suppressions, (cat. 217)
Latest restoration: 1989

**Jacopo dal Ponte, known as
Bassano,** workshop of
(Bassano c. 1510–1594)

Adoration of the Shepherds

Canvas, 120 × 222 cm
Acquisition: 1933, from the State
depository, (cat. 902)
Latest restoration: 1956

Jacopo dal Ponte, known as Bassano and assistants
(Bassano c. 1510-1594)

The Virgin and Child Enthroned in Glory with Saint Jerome

Canvas, 220 × 161 cm
Acquisition: 1930, from the state depository, (cat. 920)

Paolo Caliari, known as Veronese
(Verona 1528-1588)

Assumption of the Virgin

Canvas, 396 × 200 cm
Acquisition: 1812, following the Napoleonic suppressions, (cat. 265)
Latest restoration: 1988

Paolo Caliari, known as Veronese, workshop of
(Verona 1528-1588)

The Madonna of the Rosary

Canvas, 173 × 316 cm
Acquisition: 1844, following the Napoleonic suppressions, (cat. 207)
Latest restoration: 1986-87

Carlo Caliari
(Venice 1570-1596)

Saint Augustine Dictating his Rules to the Lateran Canons

Canvas, 285 × 146 cm
Acquisition: 1919, with the Austrian restitutions, (cat. 813)

Domenico Robusti, known as Domenico Tintoretto
(Venice 1560-1635)

Two Portraits of Confreres from the Scuola dei Mercanti

Canvas, 330 × 194 cm each
Acquisition: 1919, with the Austrian restitutions,
(cat. 872, 873)
Latest restoration: 1956

Anonymous Veneto artist
(early 17ᵗʰ century)

Young Woman playing the Guitar and Onlooker

Detached fresco, 107 × 122 cm

An Old Man and a Young Woman

Detached fresco, 106 × 122 cm
Acquisition: 1827, following its removal prior to the demolition of the building which housed it, (cat. 731, 733)
Latest restoration: 1995

Jacopo Negretti, known as Palma il Giovane
(Venice 1548-1628)

Susanna and the Old Men

Canvas, 96 × 79 cm
Acquisition: 1838, donated by Girolamo Molin, (cat. 538)
Latest restoration: 1955

The Pleasures of the Prodigal Son

Canvas, 83 × 118 cm
Acquisition: 1838, donated by Girolamo Molin, (cat. 634)
Latest restoration: 1958

Return of the Prodigal Son

Canvas, 83 × 118 cm
Acquisition: 1838, donated by Girolamo Molin, (cat. 684)
Latest restauration: 1958

The Dead Christ, Held by Three Angels

Canvas, 130 × 108 cm
Acquisition: 1850, bequest of Felicita Renier, (cat. 267)
Latest restoration: 1994

Alessandro Varotari, known as Padovanino
(Padua 1590-Venice 1650)

Frieze with Putti

Canvas, 495 × 97 cm
Acquisition: 1835, from the state depository, (cat. 802)
Latest restoration: 1962

Orpheus and Eurydice

Canvas, 164 × 119 cm
Acquisition: donated by Girolamo Contarini, (cat. 548)
Latest restoration: 1994

Francesco Maffei
(Vicenza c. 1605-Padua 1660)

The Virgin Appears to Saint Filippo Neri

Canvas, 215 × 145 cm
Acquisition: 1838, 1865 from the state depository, (cat. 1093)
Latest restoration: 1961

Charles Le Brun
(Paris 1619-1690)

The Pharisee's Banquet with Christ and Mary Magdalene

Canvas, 386 × 318 cm
Acquisition: 1815, from France in exchange for *The Wedding at Cana* by Paolo Veronese,(cat. 377)
Latest restoration: 1962

Nicola Renieri
(Nicolas Régnier, Maubeuge 1591-Venice 1667)

Allegorical Figure

Canvas, 140 × 68 cm
Acquisition: 1838, following the Napoleonic suppressions, (cat. 553)
Latest restoration: 1958

Joseph Heintz il Giovane
(Ausburg c. 1600-Venice 1678)

The Four Crowned Saints Refuse to Worship Idols

Canvas, 266 × 169 cm
Acquisition: 1982, by purchase, (cat. 1365)

Pietro Berrettini da Cortona
(Cortona 1596-Rome 1669)

Daniel in the Lions' Den

Canvas, 440 × 223 cm
Acquisition: 1829, following the Napoleonic suppressions, (cat. 754)
Latest restoration: 1955

Luca Giordano
(Naples 1634-1705)

The Deposition

Canvas, 440 × 243 cm
Acquisition: 1829, following the Napoleonic suppressions, (cat. 643)
Latest restoration: 1961-62

Giulio Carpioni
(Venice? 1613-Vicenza 1679)

The Triumph of Silenus

Canvas, 96 × 79 cm
Acquisition: 1910, donation of Giuseppe Rossi, (cat. 739)
Latest restoration: 1956

Sebastiano Mazzoni
(1611-1678)

The Mystical Marriage of Saint Catherine

Canvas, 154 × 449 cm
Acquisition: 1965, from Santa Caterina, (cat. 1331)
Latest restoration: 1956

Saint Catherine Disputing with the Philosophers

Canvas, 167 × 445 cm
Acquisition: 1965, from Santa Caterina, (cat. 1330)
Latest restoration: 1956

Giovanni Antonio Fumiani
(Venice 1650-1710)

Christ with the Doctors

Canvas, 553 × 314 cm
Acquisition: 1988, from the state depository, (cat. 1390)
Latest restoration: 1988-90

Gregorio Lazzarini
(Venice 1655-Villabona 1730)

Circumcision

Canvas, 553 × 314 cm
Acquisition: 1988, from the state
depository, (cat. 1391)
Latest restoration: 1988-90

Alessandro Magnasco
(Genoa c. 1667-c. 1749)
and **Anton Francesco Peruzzini**
(Ancona 1650/55-Milano 1720/25)

*Landscape with Praying Monks,
or The Great Wood*

Canvas, 174 × 237 cm
Acquisition: 1989, upon the
exercise of a right of pre-emption,
(cat. 1389)

Giambattista Piazzetta
(Venice 1683-1754)

*Christ Crucified with the Two
Thieves*

Canvas, 76 × 62 cm
Acquisition: 1905, by purchase,
(cat. 719)
Latest restoration: 1995

Michele Marieschi
(Venice 1710-1743)

View with Bridge

Canvas, 62 × 95 cm
Acquisition: 1908, by purchase,
(cat. 715)

Francesco Zugno
(Venice 1709-1787)

Saint Benedict

Canvas, 57,5 × 45,5 cm
Acquisition: 1977, by purchase,
(cat. 1347)
Latest restoration: 1974-75

Saint Bruno

Canvas, 57,5 × 45,5 cm
Acquisition: 1977, by purchase,
(cat. 1348)
Latest restoration: 1974-75

Giuseppe Bazzani
(Mantua 1690-1769)

Adoration of the Magi

Canvas, 106 × 79 cm
Acquisition: 1909, donated
by A. Salvadori, (cat. 747)
Latest restoration: 1938

Rest in Egypt

Canvas, 106 × 79 cm
Acquisition: 1909, donated
by A. Salvadori, (cat. 748)
Latest restoration: 1938

Francesco Hayez
(Venice 1791-Milan 1882)

Destruction of the Temple of Jerusalem

Canvas, 183 × 82 cm
Acquisition: 1868, by donation
from the artist
Latest restoration: 1989

Giambattista Mariotti
(Venice 1694-Padua c. 1765)

Saint Ignatius of Loyola Before the Pope

Canvas, 119 × 160 cm
Acquisition: 1960, by purchase,
(cat. 1321)
Latest restoration: 1960-61

Giandomenico Tiepolo
(Venice 1727-1804)

The Institution of the Eucharist

Canvas, 137 × 100 cm
Acquisition: 1807, from the old
Accademia, (cat. 488)
Latest restoration: 1960

Alessandro Longhi
(Venice 1733-1813)

The Architect Tommaso Temanza

Canvas, 72 × 55 cm
Acquisition: 1845, donated by
Francesco Lazzati, (cat. 478)
Latest restoration: 1994

Portrait of Doge Alvise IV Mocenigo

Canvas, 82 × 65 cm
Acquisition: 1807, from the old
Accademia, (cat. 473)
Latest restoration: 1958

Portrait of Doge Paolo Renier

Canvas, 81 × 66 cm
Acquisition: 1807, from the old
Accademia, (cat. 477)
Latest restoration: 1961

Madonna

Canvas, 44 × 36 cm
Acquisition: 1959, following the
Napoleonic suppressions,
(cat. 1332)
Latest restoration: 1961

Luigi Crespi
(Bologna 1708-1779)

Self-Portrait

Canvas, 114 × 95 cm
Acquisition: 1807, from the old
Accademia, (cat. 482)

Domenico Pellegrini
(Galliera Veneta 1759-Rome
1840)

*Portrait of the Engraver Francesco
Bartolozzi*

Canvas, 106 × 89 cm
Acquisition: 1834, by donation
from the artist, (cat. 453)
Latest restoration: 1958

Giovanni Migliara
(Alessandria 1785-Milan 1837)

View of a Shoreside Church

Canvas, 47 × 56 cm
Acquisition: 1903, by purchase,
(cat. 710)
Latest restoration: 1903

Select bibliography

S. Moschini Marconi, *Gallerie dell'Accademia di Venezia. Opere d'arte dei secoli XIV e XV*, Roma 1955

Id., *Gallerie dell'Accademia di Venezia. Opere d'arte del secolo XVI*, Roma 1962

Id., *Gallerie dell'Accademia di Venezia. Opere d'arte dei secoli XVII, XVIII, XIX*, Roma 1970

G. Nepi Scirè, *Storia della collezione dei disegni*, Milano 1982

G. Nepi Scirè, F. Valcanover, *Gallerie dell'Accademia di Venezia*, Milano 1985

Gallerie dell'Accademia. Acquisizioni, edited by G. Nepi Scirè, Venezia 1988

G. Nepi Scirè, *I capolavori dell'arte veneziana. Le Gallerie dell'Accademia*, Venezia 1991

Id., *Le Gallerie dell'Accademia*, Roma 1993

Id., *Le Gallerie dell'Accademia di Venezia*, Venezia 1994

Id., *Guida alla Quadreria*, Venezia 1995
(with bibliography)

and:

Giovanni Gerolamo Savoldo, exhibition catalogue, Milano 1990

Tiziano, exhibition catalogue edited by F. Valcanover, Venezia 1990

La pittura nel Veneto. Il Quattrocento, 2 voll., Milano 1990

Jacopo Bassano ca 1510-1592, exhibition catalogue edited by L.B. Berverly, P. Marini, Bologna 1992

Piero e Urbino. Piero e le corti rinascimentali, exhibition catalogue edited by P. Dal Poggetto, Venezia 1992

Andrea Mantegna, exhibition catalogue edited by S. Martineau, London 1992

Leonardo & Venezia, exhibition catalogue, Milano 1992

La pittura nel Veneto. Il Trecento, Milano 1992

Le siècle de Titien, exhibition catalogue edited by M. Laclotte, Paris 1993

Pietro Longhi, exhibition catalogue edited by A. Mariuz, G. Pavanello, G. D. Romanelli, Milano 1993

Bessarione e l'umanesimo, exhibition catalogue edited by G. Fiaccadori, Napoli 1994

Jacopo Tintoretto. Ritratti, exhibition catalogue edited by P. Rossi, Milano 1994

La pittura nel Veneto. Il Settecento, Milano 1995

Bernardo Strozzi. Genova 1581/82-Venezia 1644, exhibition catalogue edited by E. Gavazza, G. Nepi Scirè, G. Rotondi Terminiello, Milano 1995

Tiziano Amor Sacro e Amor Profano, exhibition catalogue, Milano 1995

Splendori del Settecento veneziano, exhibition catalogue, Milano 1995

Il Trecento Riminese, a cura di D. Benati, Milano 1995

Tiepolo, exhibition catalogue edited by K. Christiansen, Milano 1996

*Il soffitto degli Scalzi
di Giambattista Tiepolo,*
"Quaderno della Soprintendenza
per i Beni Artistici e Storici
di Venezia", 21, Venezia 1997

*Lorenzo Lotto il genio inquieto del
Rinascimento,* exhibition catalogue,
Milano 1997

J. Anderson, *Giorgione peintre
de la "Brièvete poetique".
Catalogue raisonné,* Paris 1996

A. Ballarin, *Jacopo Bassano. Scritti
1964-1995,* edited by V. Romani,
5 vols., Cittadella 1995

E. Battisti, *Le origini religiose
del paesaggio veneto,* in *Esistenza mito
ermeneutica. Scritti per Enrico Castelli,*
Roma-Padova 1980, I ("Archivio
di Filosofia" 1980, n. 1)

S. Campbell, *Cosmè Tura di Ferrara,*
Yale 1998

C.E. Cohen, *The Art of Giovanni
Antonio da Pordenone,*
Cambridge 1995

O. Ferrari, G. Scavizzi, *Luca
Giordano. L'opera completa,* 2 vols.,
Napoli 1992

P. Fortini Brown, *La pittura nell'età
di Carpaccio. I grandi cicli narrativi,*
Venezia 1992

M. Gemin, F. Pedrocco, *Giambattista
Tiepolo. Dipinti. Opera completa,*
Verona 1993

A. Gentili, *Giovanni Bellini,
la bottega, i quadri di devozione,*
in "Venezia Cinquecento", I, 2,
July-December 1991

Id., *Le Storie di Carpaccio. Venezia,
i turchi, gli ebrei,* Venezia 1996

R. Goffen, *Giovanni Bellini,*
Milano 1990

Id., *Titian's Women,*
New Haven-London 1997

B. Hope, *A new Documento about
Titian's Pietà,* in *Sight & Insight:
Essay on Art and Culture
in Honour of E.H. Gombrich at 85,*
London 1994

P. Humfrey, *Carpaccio. Catalogo
completo dei dipinti,* Firenze 1991

Id., *The Altarpiece in Renaissance
Venice,* New Haven-London 1993

G. Marin, *Vittore Belliniano e Lorenzo
Lotto,* "Studi di storia dell'Arte",
576, Todi 1995

G. Nepi Scirè, *Venezia e la pittura
intorno al 1500, Leonardo & Venezia,*
Milano 1992

Id., *I teleri della Sala dell'Albergo nella
Scuola di San Marco,* Venezia 1994

T. Pignatti, F. Pedrocco, *Veronese.
Catalogo completo,* 2 vols., Milano
1995

P. Rossi, *Francesco Maffei,* Milano
1991

E.A. Safarik, *Fetti,* Milano 1990

A. Scarpa Sonino, *Marco Ricci,*
Milano 1991

Id., *Jacopo Amigoni,* Cremona 1994

V. Sgarbi, *Carpaccio,* Milano 1994

D. Thiebaut, *Le Christ à la colonne
d'Antonello de Messina,* "Les Dossier
des Musée du Louvre",
Paris 1993